DATE DUE

MEDIA AND REVOLUTION

*Moulding a New Citizenry in France
during the Terror*

by James A. Leith

Canadian Broadcasting Corporation

Printed in Canada for
CBC PUBLICATIONS, BOX 500, TORONTO 1
by The Hunter Rose Company

This book contains the texts of eight half-hour radio talks first broadcast during the fall of 1967 in *Ideas*, a program series of the CBC Department of Public Affairs. The talks were organized by Phyllis Webb and produced by James Anderson.

JAMES A. LEITH is Associate Professor of French History and Deputy Chairman of the Department of History at Queen's University, Kingston. Professor Leith took an honours B.A. in Modern History at the University of Toronto, an M.A. at Duke University in North Carolina, and a Ph.D. at the University of Toronto following a year of study in Paris. He taught for three years at the University of Saskatchewan before going to Queen's in 1961, and has also been a visiting professor at Cornell University. He has done extensive research in France with assistance from the Royal Society of Canada, the Canada Council, the Humanities Research Council, and the Arts Research Committee at Queen's. His publications include *The Idea of Art as Propaganda in France: a Study in the History of Ideas*, University of Toronto Press, 1965, and numerous articles and reviews in scholarly journals.

CONTENTS

In August of 1793 France was entering its fifth year of revolution, a year fated to be remembered as the time of the Terror. French government and society had been profoundly changed since the convocation of the Estates General. The Estates, transformed into the Constituent Assembly, had approved the Declaration of the Rights of Man which affirmed the sovereignty of the people, conferred equal rights on all citizens, proclaimed the rule of law, and guaranteed liberty of thought. That Assembly had also destroyed the remnants of the manorial system, discarded titles of nobility, replaced the historic provinces with uniform departments, secularized church property, and created a national Church largely beyond papal control. Then, after more than two years of work, the Constituent Assembly had completed its design for a constitutional monarchy based on broad popular participation.

The new régime had gone into effect in October of 1791 with the meeting of the Legislative Assembly, but had survived for only ten months. Louis XVI's attempted flight even before the final draft of the constitution had been approved had weakened the régime from the start. Many members of the lower classes had felt that as yet they had few material gains to show as a result of the Revolution. The upheaval had caused economic dislocation and serious inflation. It had also bred a crop of radicals who wanted to carry the Revolution further. But it had been the advent of war with Austria and Prussia which had finally undermined the monarchy, for the king and Marie Antoinette could not disguise the fact that they sympathized with the enemy who threatened to overrun the country and punish the revolutionaries. A popular insurrection seized the palace on August 10, 1792. The Assembly was forced to call for election of a Convention to draw up a more democratic constitution for France.

This Convention had declared France a Republic on September 22, 1792. From the start, however, the new assembly had been torn by factional disputes. At first the Girondists dominated, a loose group of individualists such as Brissot, Vergniaud, Buzot, and Guadet, most of whom came from the area around Bordeaux and other provincial centres. These men were opposed by Robespierre and other radical Jacobins whose support centred on Paris. These Jacobins earned the nickname "The Mountain" because they occupied the high benches in the Convention to the left of the speaker. However, the bulk of the assembly, the so-called Plain, belonged to neither group. The Girondists had gradually lost support because of their unceasing attacks on their rivals, their deep distrust of the Paris populace, their rather equivocal policies during the trial of Louis XVI, and their reluctance to adopt the strong political and economic measures demanded by the war—a war which their leaders had warmly advocated. A Committee of Public Safety was created in April to co-ordinate the ministries, but for fear of dictatorship the Girondists had hesitated to give it real authority. Then the defection to the enemy of General Dumouriez, their friend and appointee, had further discredited them. On June 2, 1793, another Paris insurrection had forced arrest of the Girondists and brought the triumph of the Jacobins.

The Jacobins in Paris and their thousands of branch clubs in the provinces held a variety of views on politics, morality, education, and religion, but they did share certain common beliefs. The first thing the Jacobins wanted was a republican form of government. They were bitterly opposed to an hereditary ruler or aristocracy and believed that power had to be derived from the sovereign people. Most of the clubs had protested against property qualifications for voting under the first constitution and soon supported universal manhood suffrage. Also, although they developed a highly centralized government during the Terror, they retained a certain distrust of executive authority. Jacobins insisted too that the state should be secular and recognize none but laymen, and at the peak of the Terror many of them were waging a bitter war against the Catholic Church. Socially Jacobins had a mystical belief in equality, with many of them insisting that men should even be roughly alike externally—in manners, morals, dress, and language. This desire for equality extended into their economic thought where their ideal was a society of small proprietors. Often they sounded like social revolutionaries in their attacks on rich merchants and manufacturers. Finally, the Jacobins were puritans in moral matters: their Republic was to be a Republic of Virtue as severe as Calvin's Geneva.

After their triumph in June the Jacobins had hastily completed a new constitution. The new document was very democratic, with the national assembly and local officials all to be elected by universal manhood suffrage. It expanded the list of rights from seventeen to thirty-five, limiting by considerations of public interest the right to own property, and adding the rights to subsistence and to revolt against oppression. But in order not to appear too radical the Jacobins recognized the existence of a Supreme Being, granted freedom of worship, acknowledged the right to property under law, declared that morality is the foundation of society, and guaranteed the public debt. "We can now present to the universe a constitutional code, infinitely superior to all moral and political institutions," declared Robespierre at the Paris Jacobin Club, "a work doubtless capable of improvement, but which presents the essential basis of public happiness, offering a sublime and majestic picture of French regeneration." The new constitution was formally accepted by the delegates of the primary assemblies of France at a great Festival of Unity and Indivisibility on August 10, the anniversary of the overthrow of the monarchy a year earlier. The parades, ceremonies, harangues, singing, and dancing lasted more than sixteen hours. The Convention ordered that a medal designed by David be struck to commemorate the celebrations, and for months later the theatres presented dramatic representations of the festival.

In spite of all this fanfare, the constitution was not put into effect. France was engaged in a bitter war with a coalition which now included Britain, Austria, Prussia, Holland, Spain, and some smaller states. In the mid-summer of 1793 the enemy threatened to penetrate into France from the north, east, and south. Because the republican government suspected that many officers were royalist sympathizers, it considered whole units of the army useless. Then in late August Toulon, with the whole Mediterranean fleet, fell into British hands, thanks to disaffected Frenchmen. The year-old Republic also faced serious counter-revolution inside its frontiers. The widespread Federalist uprising, fanned by fleeing Girondists earlier in the summer, had proved largely ephemeral, but Bordeaux and Lyons were still in revolt. The royalist rebellion which had erupted in the Vendée region in March was contained but not suppressed. At the same time the government confronted grave economic problems. Prices had risen sharply, paper currency had lost value, employment was uncertain, and disorders throughout the country had disrupted food production. Hungry or afraid of hunger, the common people of the capital seethed with discontent, incited by the *enragés* or "enraged men" who demanded ruthless measures against profiteers, hoarders, and monopolists.

Faced with invasion, counter-revolution, and economic turmoil, the Jacobin leaders decided that to disband the Convention and to hold new elections at that time would only perpetuate anarchy and risk restoration of the monarchy. Consequently they left their new constitution in a display case in the Convention and developed an increasingly ruthless and authoritarian form of government. In October the Convention made a declaration of fundamental significance for modern times: *the provisional government of France is revolutionary until the peace*. The Convention gave notice that, instead of dissolving upon completion of its original task of drafting a constitution, it was going to continue to govern on an emergency basis. The Committee of Public Safety together with its auxiliaries, although theoretically still subordinate to the Convention, was now recognized as a government, the official executive of the nation. Until the Revolution was secure this Committee was authorized to rule by "revolutionary"—that is by exceptional and expeditious—means.

In a speech to the Convention on Christmas day, 1793, Robespierre defined the principles of *gouvernement révolutionnaire*, which he claimed was as unprecedented as the Revolution which had brought it about:

> The aim of constitutional government is to preserve the Republic; that of revolutionary government is to establish it.

4

The Revolution is the war of liberty against its enemies; the constitution is the régime of victorious and peaceable liberty.

Revolutionary government requires extraordinary activity for the very reason that it is at war. It is subject to less uniform and regular rules because the circumstances in which it finds itself are stormy and unpredictable, and because above all it is compelled to deploy novel and swift expedients to cope with new and pressing dangers.

Constitutional government devotes itself to civil liberty; revolutionary government to public liberty. Under a constitutional government it is almost enough to protect individuals from the abuses of public authority; under a revolutionary régime public authority itself is forced to resist all the factions which attack it.

Revolutionary government owes good citizens the complete protection of the nation; to the enemies of the people it owes nothing but death.

In many ways this emergency revolutionary government can be considered a prototype of the modern totalitarian state. The Committee of Public Safety steadily consolidated most power in its own hands until it exercised a degree of central authority unprecedented even among the so-called absolute monarchs of the Old Régime. Although the members of the Committee continued to believe in private property and free trade, they were also forced by economic chaos and the demands of war to preside over a dictated economy and forced mobilization the like of which was not to be seen again until the twentieth century. This was a police state operating a vast terrorist machine with the Committee of General Security at the top, the dread Revolutionary Tribunal in Paris, similar courts in some provincial centres, and watch committees in each commune and in all the wards of larger towns. And at the same time it was a single party state because the Jacobins claimed to represent the whole people who, if they really understood their common interests, could only have one will. Any group which opposed the Jacobins could be accused of acting independently of the people, of dividing and weakening them, and of pursuing the selfish interests of a faction, and consequently by definition anyone who opposed the régime was an enemy of the people.

But perhaps the most strikingly modern feature of the revolutionary government during the Terror, and the one which we intend to explore in these talks, was the attempt to mobilize all the existing mass media in a vast program of indoctrination. During the winter and spring of 1793-4 the Jacobin leaders attempted to exploit books, pamphlets, newspapers, plays, images, music, and festivals in an effort to create a like-minded citizenry from one end of France to the other. The need was urgent. Revolutionary government had been declared in the name of "the people" whom Robespierre and his colleagues conceived of in ideal terms—virtuous, patriotic, united, devoted to freedom. But the actual people of France were bitterly divided after more than four years of revolutionary change. There was no real majority in favour of anything. The ideal people did not exist: they would have to be created. Only then could the Republic be firmly established.

The Jacobin conception of sovereignty made even more pressing their need to create a like-minded citizenry. They were engaged in the attempt to transfer sovereign power from a theoretically absolute monarch to the people. Since under the Old Régime the king had claimed to exercise power as an individual moved by his personal will, radical revolutionaries thought that the new sovereign—the people—ought also to have a single will. They spoke of the people in the singular, implying an individual writ large. For men like Robespierre it followed that it was not enough in a democracy simply to compromise conflicting opinions and interests. Such a body politic would be like a man torn within himself. As a result the Jacobin leader emphasized the need for *une volonté unique*—a single will. But only a campaign of mass indoctrination could shape such a will.

The Jacobin emphasis on will rather than opinion as the basis of political authority had far-reaching and frightening consequences. If democracy must rest on a common will rather than on majority opinion, then in order to establish a democratic Republic revolutionary government had not only to inform and enlighten the people: it had to engender common motives and aspirations. But shaping men's wills rather than informing their minds involved influencing their habits, attitudes, and emotions. In short it involved a *moral* transformation. At the peak of the Jacobin propaganda campaign Barère told the Convention: "The Committee is busy with a vast plan of regeneration which ought to result in ridding the Republic simultaneously of immorality and prejudice, superstition and atheism." A campaign for moral renewal such as this would have to penetrate into every aspect of life.

The desire to achieve a moral change was intensified by the fact that Jacobinism developed into a pseudo-religion intent on converting men to its faith. The Jacobin clubs throughout France employed for their gatherings a ritual and a vocabulary not unlike that of the traditional Church. They had their revolutionary catechisms, patriotic prayers, republican hymns, purification rites, communal feasts, civic altars and temples, Trees of Liberty which substituted for crosses, processions complete with images of martyrs, and at times even consecrated burial grounds for the republican faithful. Their meetings resounded with talk of sin, heresy, salvation, regeneration, and holiness. This was not just retention of traditional vocabulary for want of something better—it revealed a genuine religiosity. Jacobin propaganda sprang partly from the proselytizing zeal of a new religion.

Many revolutionaries were certain that through proper indoctrination they could actually create a new breed of citizen. One textbook author spoke confidently of the possibility of creating *une nouvelle race*. Locke's theories of knowledge, which were very influential in eighteenth-century France, had encouraged a widespread belief in the malleability of human nature. If children were born with blank slates and all ideas entered their minds as sense impressions, then it seemed to follow that human beings could be shaped in a desirable way by exposing them to the right sort of influences from childhood onward. Speaking of the child in his crib, the author of one little civic manual wrote: "We think he is a soft wax capable of receiving whatever imprint one wishes." Not surprisingly, this propagandist believed that society could be transformed through moral regeneration.

Belief in the possibility of creating a new republican man was also encouraged by the crude associational psychology of the day. Many eighteenth-century thinkers believed that, given men's attraction to what is pleasant and their revulsion from what is unpleasant, men could be led to socially desirable goals by associating them with pleasure and approval, and away from undesirable ones by linking them with misery and opprobrium. Long before the Revolution the article "Esthétique" in one of the supplementary volumes of Diderot's great *Encyclopédie* had proposed a new science, not unlike what we would call motivation research, to discover how various sensations arouse pleasure or pain in order to apply this knowledge to derive the greatest moral utility from the various arts. Many revolutionaries were confident that by applying such a technique stories, art, music, and drama could be employed to mould good republicans on a massive scale.

Above all most revolutionaries had abandoned the Christian belief in original sin. If men were indeed unhampered by any innate perversity, and wrong-doing was the product of ignorance or mis-information, then men could be re-made through education. Many republicans believed that the natural goodness of man could lead to moral transformation if only men were rightly directed. "Since man is naturally inclined toward what is good," wrote Prévost, the author of a handbook on etiquette for young republicans, "and since he discovers evil when he strays from the route which reason maps out, it is only a matter of showing him how pleasant the way of virtue is for mankind. . . ." In introducing a decree for a textbook contest to the Convention on behalf of the Committee of Public Instruction, Grégoire likewise dismissed the notion that man was inherently evil and expressed confidence that republican education could give the future citizen *une nouvelle trempe*—a new stamp or character.

Republican pedagogues were convinced that environmental influences could be effective in creating a novel type of citizen provided that they were applied very early when the child was most impressionable. "There are two truths which it is essential to establish from the start," wrote Bulard, one of the most prolific textbook authors of the Revolution; "the first is that man is a product of his education. . . ; the second is that man is capable of being directed toward what is good from his earliest childhood. . . ." As the anonymous compiler of another civic manual expressed it, the child should imbibe love of the Fatherland and of liberty with his mother's milk. Grégoire wanted supervision by the state to commence with the very conception of the child. We shall see that much Jacobin propaganda was consciously directed at pre-schoolers and primary-school children.

In their campaign to creat a new citizenry the Jacobins were acutely conscious of the need to appeal to men's emotions and senses. This awareness lay behind the desire to mobilize *all* media, not just the printed word, but the various arts as well. "The people need songs, festivals, and spectacles," the songwriter Devienne had written back in 1790. "When one wishes to appeal to men whose imagination is lively, but whose minds are not yet sufficiently enlightened, it is through their senses that one must communicate." Jacobin propagandists made the same point repeatedly in prefaces to poems, songs, or dramas. They were well aware that each medium had its own peculiar impact on the senses and that none ought to remain unused in the campaign to create a new citizenry.

Although the revolutionaries appreciated the special impact of each medium, they would have considered Marshall McLuhan's dictum that "the medium is the message" completely wrong-headed. McLuhan sees the transforming impact in the medium itself rather than in its content, in the way the printed page or other medium alters sense ratios and patterns of perception. In contrast the Jacobins, like modern advertisers and other propagandists, were concerned with the content which each medium could convey. In the past, they argued, print and the various arts had been used to bolster superstition and tyranny. The vital need from the Jacobin viewpoint was to change the ideological content and social message of each medium. Left to itself a medium might remain or become once again a corrupting influence. Print, plays, pictures, music, and festivals would all have to be *républicanisés*.

Our talks over the following weeks about media at the peak of the French Revolution form part of a larger series on the general theme of tradition and innovation in society. Nowhere are the two more obviously interwoven than in the propaganda efforts of the Jacobins. In their most radical moments they echoed the past. We shall see that their concept of heroism was a stoic ideal derived from their classical education. We have already seen that their notion of sovereignty was influenced by the very monarchy they had overthrown. The word "regeneration" which they used to describe their ultimate goal had an obvious Christian derivation. And they were constantly trying to pour new wine into old bottles—republican ideology into catechisms, hymns, prayers, oaths, or ten commandments. Yet there was an entirely new dimension in their conception of the function of the state. Boissy d'Anglas summed it up in his *Essai sur les fêtes*, a work highly praised by some Jacobin papers, even though the author was a member of the Plain in the Convention. The state, he said, had the right to guide the activities of the individual "including his inner and private behaviour". Such a pronouncement is as modern as Mao-think.

At the peak of the Revolution French leaders wanted nothing less
than to create a new breed of citizen by a program of mass education. These leaders looked on print as one of the major means
of reaching millions of Frenchmen. In his sketch of human progress, written during the Terror, Condorcet had made the invention of printing a turning-point in history because he believed
that it ensured the ultimate conversion of mankind to enlightened
philosophy and the principles of the French Revolution. Condorcet was himself a victim of the Revolution, but his survivors
retained his faith in the potency of print. In Pierre Maréchal's
little republican almanac, in which some notable contribution to
human welfare was honoured each day, January 1 was devoted to
commemoration of the invention of printing. Even that protean
comic figure of the stage, Arlequin, turned publisher of Jacobin
propaganda. In the play *Arlequin imprimeur*, presented at the
peak of the Terror, the good-natured hero assures the audience
that he now prints only patriotic works since printers who do
otherwise are as guilty as the authors they publish.

Print was to indoctrinate the individual from childhood onward. At his parents' knee the pre-schooler would listen to tales
of republican devotion. The hero of Fréville's *Vie et mort républicaines du petit Emilien*, supposedly based on the life of the
author's own son, displayed republican sentiments even before the
Revolution. On one occasion at Versailles the child watched the
splendid entrance of the king into chapel and listened to the
exclamations of the onlookers. Afterwards Emilien, anxious to
discover what made the king different from ordinary mortals,

quizzed his mother. "But does the king go pee-pee?" he asked. "Yes, my dear, just like you." "Aha! Aha! so he goes pee-pee," the boy repeated in surprise. For Emilien Louis XVI was already simply Citizen Capet. With the coming of the Revolution and the establishment of the Republic, the little hero suggested that they could still have the fancy cake traditionally eaten at the Festival of Kings by renaming it "The Equality Cake" and cutting it in equal pieces. The child who found the bean in his piece would become president of the celebration and the toast would become "Long live the Republic!" At the time of the first levy of troops to fight royalists in the Vendée the seven-year-old republican, armed with his toy sabre and his packsack, presents himself to the head of his ward in Paris, exclaiming that he wishes to defend his mother and the Fatherland. Taken mortally ill on the day of the Festival of Reason, he sings the "Marseillaise" on his deathbed and regrets dying without being useful to his mother or the Republic. One could multiply examples of such didactic stories for children.

As the child reached school age print was to become even more important as an ideological weapon. In December, 1793, the Convention approved a free compulsory primary school system which was intended to create the foundation for a democratic society. Although the régime had neither the time nor the resources to put this mass educational system into actual operation, its plans were significant for modern times. The law declared the Rights of Man, the Constitution, and a collection of heroic or virtuous acts were to be the basic texts. Furthermore, *all* primary textbooks were to be approved by the central legislature. Subsequently the Convention opened a contest for the best elementary books including civic primers. When he proposed this contest on behalf of the Committee of Public Instruction, Grégoire emphasized the importance of influencing the child at an early age. "National education must lay hold of the newborn generation," he argued; "it must search out the infant at his mother's breast or in his father's arms in order to share their tenderness and enlighten it. The concern of the Fatherland begins when the development of a new germ promises a new individual for society." The contest was not decided until long after the overthrow of Robespierre, and by that time the whole political climate had drastically altered. But we can get an idea of the sort of techniques which advanced republicans wished to apply from examining the textbooks which were published in the Year II of the French Republic, many of which were given honourable mention by government bodies or were enthusiastically reviewed by Jacobin newspapers.

Lessons in reading could serve to convey a civic lesson providing the exercises were carefully devised. For example, the *Eléments du jeune républicain*, an anonymous work submitted to the government contest for textbooks, taught the child the alphabet and how to spell while simultaneously drilling him in republican doctrines. The book begins with the alphabet in various fonts and then teaches the child to put the letters together in syllables. The first practice piece tells about the existence of the Supreme Being whose worship had been decreed by the Convention. Later exercises dealt with Liberty and Equality, the duties and opportunities of a free man, republican virtues, civic festivals, and similar themes. Other textbooks taught reading through "conversations" about the advantages of republican government or through short moralistic stories.

As the student advanced to grammar, that too could be made to serve a dual purpose. Bulard's *Grammaire française républicaine* looked just like a traditional grammar except for the calculated choice of examples. The definite article was illustrated by such examples as "*le* républicain", "*la* vertu", "*les* moeurs", and "*les* héros". Republican, virtue, morals, heroes—a nice case of the association of ideas. The agreement of adjectives with nouns was likewise illustrated by "le *vertueux* républicain", "la *vertueuse* républicaine" and "Le riche et le pauvre sont *égaux* devant la loi". Most of the illustrations had an ideological slant down to the final example of the exclamation mark: "How sweet it is to die for the Fatherland!"

Republicans, of course, also wanted direct civic education at home and in the schools. During the Terror there was a flood of little manuals and catechisms intended to instruct children in their duties as citizens. Many were written for the textbook contest opened by the Convention. *Le manuel des jeunes républicains* by the printer Patris was typical. It opened with a collection of anecdotes about Bara, the adolescent hero of the fighting in the

Vendée region. There followed a bird's-eye-view of the history of France concluding with a panegyric on the work of the Revolution. Elsewhere the work contained a section on the essence of republican government; an account of how one acquired or lost French citizenship; the rights of man and their significance; the working of the electoral system; the powers of the various branches of the government; a gazetteer of the new departments; and a collection of heroic deeds by French republicans.

Some of the manuals featured imaginary dialogues, but most revealed their religious ancestry by their technique of question and answer. The anonymous *Alphabet des sansculottes*, for example, dealt in simple questions and answers with the duties of a republican towards the Supreme Being and his fellow citizens, the nature and form of the French government, the most glorious events of the Revolution, the most important revolutionary martyrs, and the transformation of the foreign situation under Jacobin leadership. The section on government illustrates the technique:

Q. What is the form of government?
A. Republican.
Q. What does this word mean?
A. Concern for the interests of everyone.
Q. On what is this government founded?
A. On justice.
Q. What upholds it?
A. Enlightenment and independence backed by force.
Q. What is our constitution?
A. Popular.
Q. To whom do we owe this constitution?
A. To the people and to that section of the Convention called the Mountain, the true friends of the people.
Q. What are the foundations of this constitution?
A. The rights of man, liberty and equality.
Q. Repeat the rights of man.
A. The French people. . . .

The student would then repeat the thirty-five articles of the Declaration of the Rights of Man.

The Christian legacy was even more evident in a small manual by Citizen Poitevin entitled *Catéchisme républicain* and intended specifically for children of both sexes. The catechism began with questions about the new republican sacraments:

Q. What is Baptism?

A. It is the regeneration of the French begun on July 14, 1789, and soon supported by the entire French nation.

Q. What is Confirmation?

A. It is the convocation and formation of a National Convention which, correcting the numerous mistakes of the first two assemblies, totally abolished kingship in order to substitute a republican régime.

Q. What is Communion?

A. It is the association proposed to all peoples by the French Republic henceforth to form on earth only one family of brothers who no longer recognize or worship any idol or tyrant.

Q. What is Penitence?

A. Today it is the wandering existence of traitors to their Fatherland. It is the banishment of all those monsters who, unworthy to inhabit the land of Liberty and to share the benefits which their villainy has only delayed, will soon be driven out of every corner of the globe, and, having become an abomination to all life, will have no refuge except in the bowels of the earth which they have overly polluted with their crimes.

Q. What is Extreme Unction?

A. It is the final crisis in which all the tyrants joined together, all the hired conspirators, all the assembled robbers will at last be annihilated by the spirit of Liberty and the fearless courage of the protectors of humanity. Lastly, it is the triumph of the rights of man over the insolent pretensions of despots.

Q. What is Ordination?

A. It is the rule of the laws of nature which restores to all men the right to obey the will of the Creator. It is the obliteration of those decrees which condemn to insignificance and vice a class of men destined through education to be models of all the virtues. It is reason itself which calls all creatures to heed that moving impulse which is the basis of social harmony. . . .

Q. What is Marriage?

A. It is the Social Pact which summons all human kind to enjoy untroubled the concord which the general interest dictates by proscribing forever the frightful scourge of war. It is the tacit but necessary recognition of the mutual help which all men owe one another.

This catechism then provided lists of republican sins and virtues, tables of the rights and duties of the citizens, a prayer, and ten commandments, before ending up with the "Marseillaise" and a civic oath.

The common theme of these civic handbooks was devotion to the state, subordination to the general good, and severe self-discipline. Nowhere is the puritanism of advanced revolutionaries more evident than in these little primers. Jacobin catechisms commonly contained formidable lists of republican virtues—piety toward the Deity, love of the Fatherland, affection for one's parents, obedience to the laws, good faith and sincerity, justice, beneficence, austerity, temperance, patience, courage, and love of hard work. The young Frenchman was apparently to have these moral imperatives constantly before him. A manual entitled *Pensées républicaines*, like a book of religious devotion, offered children a moralistic or patriotic adage for every day in the year:

- The welfare of the people is the supreme law.
- Under a free government one's personal interest is always found in the general good.
- The first rule of society is not to inflict harm; the second is to be useful.
- A good citizen cannot find something useful for himself which is not so for the Republic.
- If love of the Fatherland ought to be the first of our duties, it ought also to be the first of our sentiments.

The authors of these civic manuals usually sought to propagate a simple deistic religion. Most of them were viciously anti-Christian, but they were convinced that belief in a Supreme Being was necessary to provide a sanction for republican morality and a basis for social cohesion. For example, in *La Philosophie des sans-culottes*, Petterson argued that the prospect of reward or punishment in the hereafter provided a powerful incentive to virtue. The religion he taught had a simple creed—belief in a beneficent creator, an afterlife, happiness for the just, and punishment of the unjust. And worship consisted of good citizenship: "Genuine divine worship consists of being just, beneficent, and living exactly according to the laws," he wrote. Some authors were more radical and cast doubts on the immortality of the soul, but very few were willing to base republican morality on a purely secular basis.

Little handbooks appeared teaching youths a new code of manners to match this severe morality. Prévost's *Véritable civilité républicaine*, for example, counselled boys and girls to avoid the vain finery of the Old Régime and the affected speech of the former aristocracy. The author urged the young Frenchman to deport himself at all times like a staunch republican. "From childhood the republican ought to realize that a decidedly resolute bearing is the mark of his liberty," wrote Prévost. "He must not romp along giddily or drag his legs like heavy weights. May he rather walk with his body upright and an even step." Other manuals admonished the student to use "citizen" in place of "monsieur" now that an egalitarian society had replaced an hierarchical one. He was to be careful never to sign a letter "your most obedient servant", but to end with some salutation such as "your brother", "your equal" or "your fellow citizen". In addition he was never to kiss a lady's hand since such gallantry from the Old Régime was demeaning to a stalwart, manly republican.

At the peak of the Revolution republican propagandists also sought to mould the young by printing accounts of the deeds of revolutionary heroes. The most ambitious project of this kind was the periodical entitled *Recueil des actions héroïques et civiques*, compiled by the Jacobin Bourdon on orders from the Committee of Public Instruction and the Convention. The first number recounted twenty examples of republican morality in action. This collection was to be distributed to municipalities, the army, popular societies, and all schools. The story of the adolescent soldier Bara was typical of the sort of heroism which French children were expected to emulate. When he saw his commander hesitate to burn down the house which was the Bara family's sole possession, the lad himself had set it afire lest it shelter counter-revolutionaries. So that he might send home money to his poor mother, he had lived on dry bread. Finally, he had died in the Vendée at the age of twelve or thirteen, refusing to surrender to a band of royalists and defiantly shouting, "Long live the Republic!" Other typical selections recounted cases of group heroism. There were the zealous patriots in the area of the Vosges who, when horses were unavailable, yoked themselves to two forage wagons and pulled them for two days. The fifth (and last) edition of this periodical was devoted, not to isolated examples of self-sacrifice, but to the winter exploits of the French armies of the Rhine and the Moselle.

History was likewise to convey object lessons to the young republican. Many of the civic manuals and catechisms contained brief polemical histories of the Old Régime and the Revolution. In his catechism, *L'Ami des jeunes patriotes*, Chemin-Dupontès needed only a short passage to explain the coming of the Revolution:

The French people had for a long time been oppressed by a small number of individuals who had appropriated all the rights and goods of the nation; but these individuals, as stupid as they were criminal, known as kings, princes, nobles, bishops, and so on, made the people so miserable by weighing them down with taxes and vexations of all sorts that they reduced them to despair. The people, who had allowed themselves to be blinded by fanaticism, that is by religious errors, and enslaved by tyranny, finally opened their eyes. They rose up, armed themselves, destroyed the Bastille, the old stronghold of despotism, and shook the throne which was surrounded by numerous satellites. Such were the first trials which the people made of their power on July 14, 1789, three years before establishment of the Republic.

Chemin-Dupontès claimed that the capture of the Bastille might have been decisive for liberty had not some clever rascals introduced another despotic régime under the guise of patriotism. After three years of struggle between the friends of liberty and the supporters of masked despotism, the people rose a second time and overthrew the throne once and for all. Finally the people had risen again on June 2, 1793, to defeat the threat of Federalism.

Some authors sought to exploit history on a wider scale. Bulard, for example, produced a history of most of the republics which the world had seen in order to show that they led to the happiness of the people in contrast to the misery caused by monarchies. The first part of the book told how the Greeks overthrew tyrannical kings to establish flourishing republics. In ancient Athens it was the "Montagnards"—the Jacobins of their day—who championed popular government, whereas the Plain wanted an oligarchical régime and the maritime faction desired a mixed government. Finally Solon had admitted the sansculottes to the assemblies, cracked down on moderates, strictly enforced the laws, forced even rich children to learn a useful trade, and generally legislated for the happiness of the people. Unfortunately the Athenians and other Greeks eventually lost their freedom through disunity and corruption. "Frenchmen," Bulard warned, "remain forever united, forever incorruptible, and all the powers on earth will never vanquish you." The author used the history of Rome, Carthage, and various modern republics to drive home the same message.

One republican a little later even suggested that candy wrappers be used to convey lessons in citizenship to children. Fréville had culled from French poets a selection of civic maxims which he entitled *Temple de la morale*. Like many other republicans the editor emphasized the need to create a moral foundation for the state. He suggested that school teachers have their students recite one of the aphorisms from his anthology each morning, followed by a brief explanation illustrated by examples. But he hoped to reach an even wider audience quickly. "In order to make these maxims circulate more rapidly," he wrote, "perhaps one might substitute them for those meaningless mottoes which confectioners wrap around different sweets. In this way under the heading *bonbons patriotiques* our young citizens will find a course in morality in a bag of pistachios."

As the child progressed into adulthood he would continue to be bombarded with printed propaganda. The Convention printed innumerable speeches, reports, and proposals which it ordered distributed to authorities throughout France. The Jacobin clubs, which at the peak of the Terror were semi-official branches of the government, poured out pamphlets. The Paris club alone printed more than six hundred pamphlets during the Revolution and the thousands of provincial clubs imitated it on a smaller scale. Distribution of Robespierre's important report on the relation of religious and moral ideas to republican principles illustrates the diffusion of a speech through print. The speech was not only printed in several editions by the government, but a Paris publisher brought out a special edition decorated with a portrait of the Incorruptible plus two allegorical engravings.

There were, of course, republican catechisms, manuals, and books of devotion for adults. One variant of this sort of publication was the almanac which combined a calendar with some form of indoctrination. The *Almanach du républicain* by Rousseau-Jacquin and Dupin, for example, emphasized the anti-Christian intent of the new republican calendar and sought to replace Christian saints and holy days with republican heroes and commemoration of the great "days" of the Revolution. Other almanacs contained brief histories, accounts of French bravery and devotion, essays on civic virtue, didactic dialogues, or republican songs. Still other almanacs were designed especially for rural folk and combined information about weather and agricultural techniques with the usual republican propaganda. Such works were intended to carry the Jacobin credo into the home of the ordinary citizen.

Propaganda was spread too in the guise of poetry. Thomas Rousseau, archivist of the Jacobin club and editor of its newspaper, produced a long poem entitled *Les Crimes de la monarchie* recounting the vices of the Old Régime, the overthrow of the monarchy, and the new morality which would ensure the survival of the French Republic. Citizen Pagès published an even longer poem—ten cantos totalling 155 pages—celebrating the arrival of a new era in the history of mankind. In a review, the newspaper *Le Batave* called it a "sparkling work" and predicted it would become the epic poem of free peoples, which only proves once again how wrong critics can be. Many shorter poems were printed praising Liberty and Equality, celebrating revolutionary heroes, or exalting in the victories of French armies. Even the thirty-five articles of the Declaration of the Rights of Man were turned into verse in order that people could memorize them more easily.

Much of this propaganda was turned out spontaneously by authors and printers producing for the market. The government, however, appealed repeatedly to authors to write republican works, subsidized certain books, or gave them its warm approval once they had appeared. Also we must remember that authors and publishers were producing at a time when the slightest suspicion of opposition to the government might prove fatal. The famous Law of Suspects passed on September 17, 1793, which organized the machinery of the Terror, specifically listed as suspected persons those who *by their writings* showed themselves to be "enemies of liberty"—a phrase vague enough to make any author wary. And on June 30, 1794, the Committee of Public Safety ordered that all publications be examined by the Commission of Public Instruction. "All authors and editors will send to the Commission three copies of their works before putting them on sale," declared the decree. Even book pedlars and newsmongers were placed under surveillance of the Commission. And, as we have seen, the government intended that all textbooks used in the primary schools would be selected by the government and would include civic primers. Thus at the peak of the Terror the revolutionary government sought to ensure that print would contribute to creation of a zealous citizenry united by a single will.

There was one important form of print which we did not discuss in our talk last week because it deserves special attention—the newspaper. French revolutionaries from the beginning had revealed their awareness of the power of this medium of propaganda. "We need some means other than pamphlets to instruct all Frenchmen, ceaselessly, cheaply, and in a form which does not weary them," Brissot had written in announcing his paper *Le Patriote français* back in April, 1789. "This means is a political journal or a gazette; it is the sole vehicle of instruction for a numerous nation, limited in its resources, little accustomed to reading, and which wishes to escape from ignorance and slavery." Brissot had been devoured by the Revolution, but the Jacobins who were ascendant during the Terror likewise believed in the effectiveness of the periodical press. For this reason they were anxious to guide and direct its use.

During the Terror direction of the press came in two principal forms, one negative and one positive. Negative control came in the form of suppression of all newspapers hostile to the régime. The Jacobins destroyed the opposition press while continuing to pay tribute to the principle of freedom of the press which had been established earlier by the Constituent Assembly and had produced a proliferation of journals of all sorts. In silencing opposition newspapers and journalists Jacobins claimed to be frustrating counter-revolution, not violating basic liberty of the press. But the effect was the same. After the purge of the Girondists from the Convention the moderate press was destroyed. Journalists, printers, and newsvendors paid for their opinions with their lives and, as under the Old Régime, their publications were sometimes burned at the foot of the scaffold by the executioner. When Camille Desmoulins called for moderation of the Terror in his *Vieux Cordelier* during the winter of 1793-4, he managed to publish only six numbers and he and his wife ended up under the guillotine.

Positive direction came in the form of secret backing of one newspaper as a vehicle for government views, plus covert subsidization of about a dozen other journals. In August of 1793 the Convention gave the Committee of Public Safety a special fund of fifty million *livres*. The Committee decided to use part of this sum to shape public opinion through creation of a newspaper, but to obscure its role it chose a paper already in existence for over a month, Rousselin's *Feuille du salut public*. Later, to further mask the official character of this paper, the Committee forbade any journal from using the title "Public Safety". Rousselin substituted the word "Republic", but his journal remained the mouthpiece of the government. In addition the Committee and the Ministry of War supported other papers with subscriptions ranging from six hundred to five thousand copies each for distribution to the departments or the army.

The prospectus of the *Feuille du salut public* shows clearly the objectives of the editors, objectives which the Committee of Public Safety evidently shared. In their desire to create united support for the régime the editors advocated what we would call a single-party state, but which they preferred to call a no-party state. The dominant Jacobin politicians claimed that they represented all the people and that opposition groups consisted of selfish factions which created dissension within the Republic. "The title alone of *Public Safety* which we give to our sheet requires us not to belong to any party," wrote the editors; "for it is not through parties that the common weal will be preserved. For that, reason and virtues are needed, and parties have only expedients, hatred, and mistaken sagacity."

The prospectus also reveals that the editors believed that the citizen ought never to be able to escape from republican indoctrination. In order to engender simple morals and energetic virtues the editors promised to treat everything from a single point of view, not just in their reports about important events and decrees of the Convention, but even in their articles on the fine arts and philosophy. Their pronouncement raises the spectre of modern totalitarianism:

> We will show his Fatherland to the citizen ceaselessly, in his laws, in his games, in his home, in his loves, in his festivities. We will never leave him to himself alone. We will by this continual coercion awaken ardent love for the Fatherland. We will direct his inclination toward this single passion. It is in this way that the Frenchman will acquire a national physiognomy; it is in this way that, by identifying him so to speak with the happiness of his country, we will bring about this vitally necessary transformation of the monarchical spirit into a republican spirit. . . .

This four-page paper, which came out every morning, devoted most of its space to proceedings of the Convention and the Paris Commune, news from the departments, and some foreign reports. A series entitled "Réflexions de l'observateur des groupes" and a feature called "Variétés", provided editorial comment on a wide range of current issues. The paper published the major speeches by Robespierre and others on the Committee of Public Safety defending revolutionary government, justifying the Terror, and explaining major legislation. Occasionally the editor-in-chief did a special piece such as his vicious little essay entitled "Royalisme" ending with a blood-chilling cry, *"O lepidum caput,* oh what a splendid guarantee is the head of a tyrant cut off by the national axe!" And sometimes the paper enlivened its pages with republican poems, patriotic songs, or satirical dialogues.

The fictitious dialogue between Pitt and George III about the situation in France is vivid evidence of the anti-British propaganda common at this time in the semi-official press. Since the outbreak of war with Britain in February, 1793, hatred of British leaders had mounted steadily. Britain, which earlier in the century had been admired by some French reformers for her political freedom and religious toleration, now appeared to French republicans as a dangerous counter-revolutionary power. In the last half of the dialogue, published in late September of 1793, King George queries his Prime Minister about the economic situation in France which was under blockade by the British navy:

G. Well come on, speak to me frankly: that will be a change.

P. I was saying that the French can forego foreign trade. That is an advantage which they have over us and that is quite in keeping with their political existence. Would you believe it, Sire, that they expect to bring about the fond hope of equality? that they no longer want any rich or poor? that they mean that everybody is to eat and to be clothed through work?

G. What madness!

P. Right, but at least isn't it a beautiful madness?

G. It isn't ugly, but—for everyone to eat and be clothed, really that is an impropriety—Besides, that's impossible without foreign trade.

P. Yes, for your excellent Majesty, but not for the French. Candidly, let us agree, Sire, that external trade is all for the advantage of the rich whose possessions it increases. The poor man has few wants and is satisfied with the products of the land he inhabits. If they are plentiful he obtains them at a moderate price. What is the effect of commerce, supposing there is an abundance of such basic provisions as grain and wine and so on? It grabs part of these and, thus pushing up the price of what is left, it forces the poor to excessive toil in order to afford it. For example, France produces almost enough wine for everyone to drink it moderately: yet three-quarters scarcely know its name, because what is surplus *for the rich but not for the poor* is exported. It seems to me, Sire, that the wine produced in France ought to be reserved for the use of Frenchmen. In countries where there are few commercial markets the people are happy. They have little money but lots of provisions. Commerce wrests from the poor grain and wine with which they feed themselves, in order to exchange it for nutmegs which they don't eat.

G. Confound it, Mr. Pitt! How you do go on. I see that we must suppress French papers. They would corrupt angels. I won't hide from you, Mr. Pitt, that you have put me in a very bad temper, and if I wasn't afraid of the loud noise I would go hunting.

P. Ah, Sire, do not crush me with your august anger. What I said came from my head only. I have a heart worthy of a king. I hate the French as much as they despise me, especially since the decree which declares me an enemy of the human race. That decree ought to reassure your Majesty about me and I will make every effort to justify it.

G. Very good, Mr. Pitt. Let us forget these rebellious people and get to work.

P. But, Sire, when we work we will have to talk about the French.

G. In that case I'm going hunting.

•   •   •

Another little dialogue, this time between an old priest and a younger one, dramatizes the anti-Catholic tone of the press during the Terror. The Civil Constitution of the Clergy, passed back in 1790, had driven many priests into opposition to the

Revolution by virtually turning the Church into a government department. The outbreak of a serious counter-revolutionary movement in the Vendée appeared partly a result of clerical intrigue. In any case the Church, even the new Constitutional Church, seemed inextricably associated with the practices and attitudes of the Old Régime. Besides, the Revolution had become a new faith, and like many new religions, intolerant of old beliefs. In the dialogue, which appeared in November, 1793, the older priest attacks his young colleague who has just got married:

O.P. You are a schismatic.

Y.P. No, because I side with the great social family.

O.P. You are unworthy to be a priest.

Y.P. So I don't intend to be one much longer.

O.P. If each of us did the same who would pray for the faithful?

Y.P. No one, which would lead the faithful to pray themselves.

O.P. Who would sing praises unto the Lord?

Y.P. Those who wanted to praise the Lord.

O.P. Who would hear confession?

Y.P. They would do the same as in the early days of Christianity, men would confess to each other.

O.P. Who would say mass?

Y.P. Christ never instituted it.

O.P. Who would conduct marriages?

Y.P. The municipal officials.

O.P. Who would baptize people?

Y.P. Anybody who came along. The church gives the power to do so to everyone.

O.P. Who would bury the dead?

Y.P. That is a matter for the police.

O.P. According to you the people could therefore do without priests?

Y.P. Just as easily as they dispense with nobles and kings.

O.P. And to what would you reduce religion?

Y.P. To morality.

O.P. But if morality is embodied in our Laws and in our institutions will not religion become useless?

Y.P. Absolutely. To love one's country, to serve it, to be just to one's fellow citizens, that is to perform what is most pleasing to men and God.

O.P. So you don't want men to pray to him?

Y.P. I won't prevent it, but I find it insulting to him. It assumes that he is weak and mistrusts his justice.

O.P. You are an innovator.

Y.P. No, because I thought this way back when there were chief almoners and cardinals.

O.P. God will punish you.

Y.P. He is indeed the master, but I revere him too much to fear him.

O.P. What, no more priests!

Y.P. I don't say that we must have none. I say that we could do without them.

O.P. The deuce! That is precisely what one must not say for, if people think they can do without them, you will see that they will dispense with them.

Y.P. That will be a misfortune for priests but that is all.

O.P. You are an irreligious fellow, an atheist, and you will be sorry for having contributed to the misfortune of Frenchmen in the next world.

Y.P. I shall console myself with seeing them free and happy in this one.

In November, 1793, this paper published an interesting article addressed to republican women. It asserted that the Revolutionary Tribunal had recently provided women with a lesson which it hoped would not be missed by them. The Tribunal had condemned Marie Antoinette who had carried into France the vices of the Austrian royal family. According to this article, she had sacrificed her husband, her children, and her adopted country to the ambitions of the House of Austria. A bad mother, a debauched wife, she had died burdened with the curses of those whose ruin she had sought to consummate. Following a similar denunciation of two other victims of the guillotine, the dramatist Olympe de Gouges and Madame Roland, the paper drew a moral for housewives. If they wanted to be republicans, women would have to obey the laws and teach them to their families, seek glory in virtuous deeds, dress simply, and work hard in the home. And if they went to popular assemblies, it should never be to speak, but simply to set a good example.

In the spring of 1794 under the heading "Morale politique" the paper published editorials about such matters as how the Republic would contribute to human happiness, the nature of genuine patriotism, and the claims of the Fatherland on the individual. The paper constantly argued that the claims of the nation transcended all personal attachments and affections. Take for example the very revealing editorial entitled "La Patrie et non les individus" which appeared in an April number. Love of one's country, the article asserted, must be an exclusive passion. Then it continued:

The people are everything. For their welfare the sacrifice of the dearest affections ought never to be postponed an instant. Virtue, the very foundation of republics, is not a soft quality which everyone makes up according to his fancy out of the demands of gratitude, friendship, or nature. These are feeble ties when a more sacred obligation—the only inviolable one—demands that they be broken: namely the necessity to prove oneself a citizen. Can the fate of a man, whoever he may be, even the man whom one admires and cherishes the most, counterbalance the fortunes of the nation?

The *Feuille du salut public* also published numerous reviews and notices of books, prints, and plays. While it demanded literary and artistic skill as well as republican zeal, it bitterly denounced those whose work seemed to reflect nostalgia for the Old Régime or even a desire for political moderation. Its reviews contended that everything which was not clearly for the Revolution was necessarily against it. Moderation was denounced as a hideous vice since it implied either hypocrisy or extreme egoism. In reviewing Maréchal's blood-thirsty drama, *Le Jugement dernier des rois*, the paper expressed satisfaction that the Théâtre de la République seemed filled with tyrannicides. "At last public spirit exists," the review stated, "but it can only be sustained by turning men's minds *solely* toward the revolution, by men becoming imbued with the severe principle that *whatever seeks to distract from the common weal is subject to the jurisdiction of the Revolutionary Tribunal.*" Such pronouncements in the press must have done much to keep authors and artists in line.

The *Journal de la Montagne,* mouthpiece of the Paris Jacobin Club, was another daily subsidized by the revolutionary government. It began publication on June 1, 1793, at the very moment the Girondists were being expelled from the Convention and the Jacobins were emerging triumphant. The prospectus for the new paper emphasized the importance of shaping public opinion on which the whole success of the Revolution depended. It claimed that enemies of the Revolution had succeeded in misleading many citizens, in creating divisions among them, and in alienating the provinces from Paris. The Jacobins had decided that the best way to enlighten public opinion was to publish a journal expounding true revolutionary principles and free from corruption. The paper would print the debates of the Assembly, but would always strive to depict the opposing sides in such a way that the people would be able to distinguish their friends from their enemies. This paper then frankly aimed at moulding the mind of the masses by carefully editing the news.

Like other semi-official papers during the Terror this journal devoted much of its space to the proceedings of the Convention and the Paris Commune, to major decrees or reports, and to long lists of the sentences imposed by the Revolutionary Tribunal. Understandably it gave prominence to the activities of the Jacobin Club and to correspondence or petitions from sister clubs in the provinces. News from outlying areas and the armies on the frontiers was generally provided by reports from representatives on mission or army officers. Fiery editorials stressed the need to crush Federalism, to implement the *levée en masse* or mass mobilization, to purge political bodies of false patriots, and to sustain the Terror. The paper spiced its contents with occasional revolutionary songs, republican poems, and accounts of patriotic devotion. And in its reviews and notices it kept constant pressure on authors and artists to support Jacobin ideology.

As the de-Christianization campaign mounted in the autumn of 1793 the *Journal de la Montagne* supported the attack on Catholicism, or "superstition" as it called it, but warned of the dangers of atheism. The editor argued that if one denied the existence of a supreme intelligence then nature was reduced to chance combinations of matter in motion and no longer provided a basis for eternal moral principles. If the Girondists had believed that equality of rights was grounded in the immutable truths of nature, they would never have thought of handing over the right to govern Frenchmen to a York or some other individual to pass down from father to son. "The very idea of such a monstrosity would have made them tremble"; claimed the editor: "but I can easily imagine that such an idea might spring up in the mind of someone who does not recognize a supreme intelligence and who regards the universe as a product of accidental combinations." The paper favoured teaching children a simple deistic religion as the foundation for republican morality.

The *Journal des hommes libres,* was likewise subsidized by the revolutionary government, and was one of the papers distributed to the army. It generally featured a brief summary of foreign and domestic news, followed by long reports of the proceedings of the Convention, important laws and decrees, accounts of the Commune and the Jacobin Club, and special items and correspondence from the provinces. Like most of these papers it did not include engravings or caricatures—probably because they would have cost too much—but sometimes it printed a song, a satirical dialogue, or a brief story of republican heroism. Although it published few reviews of books or dramas, it was a strong advocate of political commitment by songwriters, playwrights, and other authors. And in its editorials it went even further than most of the semi-official press in advocating substitution of a republican moral code for Christian practices and beliefs. The paper urged its readers to be just, humane, devoted to freedom and equality, anxious to serve their fellow citizens, and utterly committed to the Fatherland. "But don't speak any longer of divinity, worship, religion or gospel," one editorial demanded. "All these words and others like them ought to be proscribed from the republican language, along with such words as king, lord, crown, etc." Robespierre and his colleagues would have retained belief in a divinity, an impersonal Supreme Being, but they too shared the hope of creating a new republican cult.

Evidently the government considered another daily, the *Journal universel,* a useful weapon in its arsenal since it assisted this paper in various ways. The editor, Audouin, seems to have written most of this little paper himself. It consisted of reports of the proceedings in the Convention, summaries of events in the capital especially the activities of the Jacobin Club, news and correspondence from the provinces, plus comments on current issues by the editor. It did not publish dialogues, poems, songs, or theatrical reviews, but the editor supplied enough vitriol to enliven the paper. Audouin was a vigorous defender of revolutionary government and terror, constantly warning of the dangers of moderation and soft-heartedness. "The revolutionary government has been our salvation," he thundered; "it will succeed in delivering us again and in ridding us of all those vile intriguers, ambitious fellows, royalists, and counter-revolutionaries who at this moment are playing their last cards. We must be careful then, not only not to stop it, but not even to slacken it for a moment."

The government subsidized and helped to distribute a number of other papers. The *Anti-fédéraliste* was founded with the special purpose of uniting all the Jacobin clubs throughout

France and of giving the public a true picture of their activities. The *Journal militaire* published all the laws and decrees concerning the armed forces, rousing proclamations by the Convention on the occasion of some notable victory, plus occasional inspirational accounts of heroism by French soldiers. The Committee of Public Safety and the ministry of war also assisted the *Batave*, the *Feuille du cultivateur*, the *Père Duchesne*, the *Républicain français*, the *Rougyff*, and the *Moniteur*. Since the latter paper had served previous régimes, it was warned that its subsidy would end if it "ceased to be composed in keeping with the republican revolution and according to the principles of liberty and equality".

These revolutionary papers played a vital role during the Terror in uniting republicans against the foreign coalition and behind the revolutionary government. In the provinces some departmental administrations subsidized and distributed regional papers to propagate republicanism. For example, the General Council of the department of the Meurthe subsidized the *Journal républicain* published at Nancy, which it sent to all the districts, communes, and popular societies in its jurisdiction. It suggested that this lively Jacobin paper be read publicly immediately after the laws. This suggestion indicates the way by which the revolutionary press influenced a wider public. Newspapers were read aloud at public gatherings, political clubs, and cafés. Print became oral to reach at least some of the illiterate or semi-literate masses.

In the spring of 1794 the revolutionary government tightened its control and direction of newspapers. After the execution of the Hébertists and Dantonists in late March and early April the last breath of liberty of the press was smothered. The Law of 22 Prairial—the tenth of June by the old calendar—defined enemies of the people in even broader terms than previous legislation. Then at the end of June, as we have mentioned before, the Committee of Public Safety ordered all publishers of periodicals and other works to send three copies for screening by the Commission of Public Instruction before putting them on sale. Meanwhile the Committee passed numerous orders to ensure the distribution of approved newspapers. And just a few weeks before the overthrow of Robespierre the Committee created a new periodical, *La Soirée du camp,* for distribution to the army and administrative authorities. The Committee requisitioned the necessary printers, ordered 10,000 copies per day, and authorized a monthly indemnity for the editors. Newspapers were obviously considered a vital weapon in the campaign to create a new French citizenry.

We have seen how during the Terror French revolutionaries poured out books, pamphlets, and newspapers aimed at indoctrinating a mass public. Nevertheless they were acutely aware of the shortcomings of print, both because many people were still illiterate and because the printed word had only a limited appeal to the senses. On the other hand the theatre could reach the illiterate and could appeal powerfully to the eye and the ear. In the course of the eighteenth century various reformers— Voltaire, Diderot, Mercier, and others—had noted the emotional appeal of drama and had advocated transformation of the theatre into an instrument for civic education. Five years before the outbreak of the Revolution the long run of Beaumarchais' *Le Mariage de Figaro* at the Comédie française had illustrated the capacity of drama to convey new ideas. Then the production of numerous didactic plays during the first four years of the Revolution had further demonstrated the potentialities of drama as an instrument of propaganda.

A long article in the *Feuille de salut public*, that covert organ of the Committee of Public Safety, reveals the Jacobin view of the theatre during the autumn of 1793. The author contended that under the Old Régime most comedies had been a mixture of pointless intrigues and crude indecencies. Almost all tragedies had preached love of kings and what had passed for "national plays" had depicted Frenchmen grovelling before arrogant monarchs. According to the author, in the early days of the Revolution the government had still tolerated dangerous plays depicting impudent royalism and guileful moderantism at grips with virtuous patriotism. The theatres no longer showed crowned vice triumphing over unfortunate virtue, or the people degraded crawling before insolent masters, but he wondered whether all the dangerous elements had yet been uprooted. He argued that all plays ought to be either patriotic or moral and called for suppression of all pointless dramas, all scandalous farces, all spectacles which debased human nature by showing masters cuffing their servants. There were no longer any valets because there were no longer any masters in the French Republic. Theatre must become a genuine school of morality teaching all the social virtues. Every day at the theatre the citizen should be inspired by the spectacle of the great epochs of the Revolution and acts of heroism. "Legislators, magistrates of the people, you who ought to direct public opinion," the author concluded; "I present you with a powerful motive force. May you know how to use it."

Jacobins did indeed learn how to employ the theatre for their purposes. The Constituent Assembly had freed the theatres from the monopolistic privileges of the king's actors and from royal censorship. The result was a proliferation of new theatres and an outpouring of new plays. At the peak of the Revolution Paris had more than forty theatres presenting hundreds of new productions a year. But during the Terror the theatre was once again subjected to censorship in various forms. To begin with there was unofficial censorship by audiences, newspapers, and political clubs. The theatre was especially vulnerable to this sort of censorship because it was the most public of the arts. Zealous republicans in the audience sometimes interrupted plays to condemn or laud the sentiments being expressed. The Jacobin Club and popular societies in the wards of the capital kept a watchful eye on the stage. For example, in September of 1793 a soldier protested ineffectually against some lines in François de Neufchâteau's *Paméla* at the Théâtre de la Nation, as the Comédie française was now called. But he then appealed successfully to the Jacobin Club which led the Committee of Public Safety to arrest the authors and actors and to close the theatre. At the same time some Jacobin newspapers railed against plays that seemed too moderate or too tolerant of the customs of the Old Régime. In such circumstances adaptability was the only way for authors, producers, and actors to survive. "Actors became weathercocks," the actor Fleury wrote later in his memoirs.

In addition there was official censorship not unlike that of the Old Régime. At first the main demand for censorship came from the Paris Commune or municipal government. Early in 1793 the Commune sought to suppress Laya's *L' Ami des lois,* ostensibly because it caused public disturbances but really because it was anti-Robespierrist. The Convention, still controlled by the Girondists, forbade this censorship although the play was discontinued because of the danger of new disorders. But in August the Convention, now dominated by Jacobins, authorized supervision of theatres by municipal authorities. "Any theatre which presents plays tending to deprave public opinion or awaken the shameful superstition of royalism will be closed," the Convention proclaimed, "and the directors will be arrested and punished according to the severity of the law." The Commune soon appointed the necessary censors who sometimes forbade plays or demanded changes. Authors and directors often submitted plays for approval before presentation. Then in March of 1794 the Commune ordered all theatres to submit their repertories for screening. And in May the Commission of Public Instruction, recently created by the Convention, likewise began investigating the repertories of all theatres. Out of 151 plays examined over a three-month period, thirty-three were rejected and twenty-five were modified. Meanwhile in Bordeaux, in Marseilles, and other provincial cities representatives on mission and local zealots censored plays and purged theatres.

The Jacobins also attempted positive encouragement of revolutionary theatre. At the same time that it authorized municipal censorship in August of 1793 the Convention ordered that certain theatres, to be selected by the Minister of the Interior, were to present during the next three months republican tragedies such as *Brutus, Guillaume Tell,* or *Caïus Gracchus* and other plays calculated to foster the principles of liberty and equality. Once a week these theatres were at government expense to offer free performances of one such play, evidently to make the theatre accessible to poorer citizens. The following March the Committee of Public Safety carried this idea further by ordering conversion of the deserted Théâtre de la Nation into a theatre for the people. The municipality was empowered to order companies from various Parisian theatres to give performances in turn three times a *décade,* as the new ten-day republican week was called. A suitable repertory of revolutionary plays was to be selected for presentation at this Théâtre du Peuple. Nor did the Committee confine its attention solely to Paris. It ordered other municipalities where a play-house existed to organize civic performances to be given free to the people each *décade.* "Only patriotic plays, chosen from a repertory approved by the municipality shall be given," the decree declared, "under surveillance of the district, answerable in turn to the Committee of Public Safety."

Positive direction also came in the form of subsidization of some theatres, purchase of multiple copies of certain plays, and occasional orders that a certain play be performed. In October of 1793 the Committee of Public Safety granted the Opera 150,000 *livres* on condition that "the administration of this theatre be based on economic principles and patriotic views, that it purchase republican works, that it perform only patriotic plays, that its repertory be purified, that it provide free presentations each week, and that for menial chores it employ parents of volunteers serving on the frontiers". The Opera was compensated for its free presentations and for performing plays imposed by the government such as *L'Inauguration de la république française, La Journée du dix août 1792,* or *Brutus.* The Théâtre des sans-culottes, the Théâtre de la République, and some others got assistance for presenting revolutionary dramas. Many authors pleaded for government assistance and some succeeded. Saulnier, Lemierre, Chénier, Bouquier, Moline, and other playwrights received government support in some form.

During the Jacobin dictatorship French classical dramas fell out of favour. The works of Corneille, Racine, Molière, and even Voltaire, became suspect. Racine's plays were purged of now unacceptable lines about monarchy. The actor Molé was charged with revising Molière's *Tartuffe,* ridding it of references to the court, suppressing entire passages, and introducing new tirades. Even Voltaire's *La Mort de César* was given a new republican ending and Anthony's speech removed. Many classics were suppressed altogether or simply abandoned. In their place came a deluge of republican works of every genre—didactic historical dramas, moralistic domestic plays, pieces celebrating recent victories, patriotic vaudevilles, great allegorical spectacles, and revolutionary ballets and operas. As some Jacobin critics admitted, many of these plays showed signs of hasty composition, but they did represent a concerted effort to mould mass sentiment.

Historical dramas now featured republican heroes rather than kings—Scaevolus, Caïus Gracchus, Spartacus, Regulus, or Brutus. In these historical plays the Jacobins did not object to some misrepresentation of the past provided it served a worthy purpose. For example Legouvé distorted history in his *Epicharis et Néron*, a five-act tragedy in verse presented at the Théâtre du Vaudeville in February, 1794. Originally the playwright had portrayed Epicharis more as history depicts her, driven to conspire against Nero because of her rage at being displaced as his mistress. But Legouvé revised his drama to give his heroine a nobler motive, turning her into a champion of liberty. "This inaccuracy is quite excusable for it is directed toward a moral and political goal," wrote the critic in the *Feuille du salut public*; "it is even praiseworthy since it gives scope for republican truths which have been felt as forcefully as they have been presented."

At the same time republican playwrights idealized contemporary heroes such as Marat, Lepelletier, Beaurepaire, Viala, and Bara. The life, death, and apotheosis of Marat inspired many plays, but in the spring of 1794 it was the teenage heroes Viala and Bara who became favourites. The revolutionary government encouraged veneration of these young martyrs because they seemed to provide ideal behavioural models for French youths. Again Jacobins were less concerned with the accuracy of the facts than with the inspiration they hoped to convey. In Briois' play, *La Mort du jeune Barra* [sic], the action opens with old Gilbert and his wife making clothing for republican soldiers. Gilbert would like to kill a couple of counter-revolutionaries before he dies, but he is too feeble to realize this dream. But Bara, a young hussar, who comes to the Gilbert house as a guest, kills six counter-revolutionaries in a single morning, and Aimée, Gilbert's daughter, bags three more. With so much in common, Bara and Aimée fall in love. Gilbert approves the match, but young Bara has to go off to battle, where, after heroic feats, he is mortally wounded. Carried back to the Gilbert house, he revives long enough to exclaim, "Let us accept our fate, Aimée. I have deserved you. I die worthy of my country, I die content. Long live the Republic!"

There was also a large number of dramas and comedies idealizing republican morality in everyday life. The common people were depicted as virtuous and patriotic—fathers and mothers who gladly see their sons volunteer to fight the enemies of the Republic, sons who waive exemptions and leave their fiancées to save the Fatherland, daughters who sacrifice the linens in their trousseaux to provide bandages for the army, and shopkeepers who refuse to raise prices even before imposition of price controls. The greatest heroism was to sacrifice personal affections for the sake of the state. The hero of a play by Pompigny entitled *L'Epoux républicain* turns his wife and son over to the Revolutionary Tribunal when he discovers they are plotting to flee from France with a former priest. "Can you desire the death of your wife? Of your son?", asks the priest. "It is nothing to me, for they deserve it," the husband replies. One critic hailed this republican husband as an admirable new character destined for a lasting place in the theatre.

The Terror produced as well some extreme anti-monarchical dramas. One of the most bloodthirsty was Maréchal's prophetic one-act play entitled *Le Jugement dernier des rois*, which opened at the Théâtre de la République just two days after the execution of Marie Antoinette. The setting is a desolate volcanic isle where sans-culottes—staunch republicans from the lower classes—representing various European nations have brought their former rulers to abandon them forever. The leader is a Frenchman even though he has no king to deposit. On the island the sans-culottes come across a motto scrawled on a rock:

BETTER A VOLCANO THAN A KING AS A NEIGHBOUR

The sans-culottes applaud this slogan which they discover is the work of an old Frenchman exiled on this island twenty years before for protesting too vigorously against the abduction of his daughter by the king. After hearing the old man's story, the French sans-culotte brings him up to date on changes in France

and his German colleague tells how they spread to other parts of
Europe:

FRENCH SANS-CULOTTE   Now listen and learn that you have been
revenged. To tell you everything would take too long. Here is the
essence: Good old chap, you have before you a representative of
each of the nations of Europe which are free and republican, for
you must realize there are no more kings in Europe.

OLD MAN   Is this true? Can it be possible?—You make sport with a
poor old man.

FRENCH SANS-CULOTTE   True sans-culottes respect old age and do
not make fun of it—as the empty courtiers of Versailles, Saint-
James, Madrid, and Vienna used to do.

OLD MAN   What! There are really no more kings in Europe?—

FRENCH SANS-CULOTTE   You will see them all disembark here. In
their turn, as you once did, they follow us in the hold of a little
armed frigate which we have outrun in order to prepare their
lodgings. You will see them all here, with one exception, however.

OLD MAN   And why this exception? One of them was scarcely worth
more than the others.

FRENCH SANS-CULOTTE   Right you are—except one, because we have
guillotined him.

OLD MAN   "Guillotined" . . . what does that mean?

FRENCH SANS-CULOTTE   We will explain that to you along with lots
of other things. We chopped off his head in the name of the law.

OLD MAN   So the French have finally become men!

FRENCH SANS-CULOTTE   Free men. In short France is a republic in
the full sense of the word. The French people have risen up. They
said "We do not want a king" and the throne vanished. They said
again, "We want a republic," and there we were, all republicans.

OLD MAN   I never dared to hope for such a revolution, but I can
imagine it. I always thought privately that the people, just as powerful as the god one preached to them, had only to express their will
—How happy I am to have lived long enough to learn of such a
great event. Oh my friends, my brothers, my children, I am in
raptures!—But so far you have told me only about France, and if
I heard correctly the first time, it appears to me that all Europe
has been delivered from the contagion of kings.

GERMAN SANS-CULOTTE   The example of the French bore fruit,
although not without difficulties. All Europe aligned against her,
not the people, but those monsters who insolently called themselves
"sovereigns". They armed all their slaves and tried every means to
break up this nucleus of liberty which Paris had established. At first
people unfairly slandered this generous nation which was first to do
justice to its king. Men tried to moderate it, federalize it, starve it,
to enslave it in a fine manner so as to repel men forever from the
régime of self-government. But by dint of reflecting about the sacred
principles of the French Revolution and reading about the sublime
deeds and heroic virtues to which it gave rise, the other peoples
said to themselves: but we are certainly dupes to let ourselves be
led to the slaughter like sheep. . . . Let us fraternize instead with

our elders in reason and in liberty. As a result every part of Europe sent brave sans-culottes to Paris to represent it. There a great assembly of all peoples agreed that on a certain day all Europe would rise in a body and free itself. In fact a general and simultaneous revolution broke out in all the countries of Europe. Each of them had its July 14 and October 5, 1789, its August 10 and September 21, 1792, its May 31 and June 2, 1793. We will teach you about these epochs, the most astonishing in all history.

OLD MAN   What marvels—Right now satisfy my impatient curiosity on one point only. I hear you all repeat the word "sans-culotte". What does this singular and striking expression mean?

FRENCH SANS-CULOTTE   That's for me to tell you. A sans-culotte is a free man. A patriot above all. The mass of real people, always good, always wholesome, is made of sans-culottes. They are all unblemished citizens, all close to poverty, who eat bread earned by the sweat of their brow, who love work, who are good sons, good fathers, good husbands, good kinsfolk, good friends and good neighbours, but as jealous of their rights as of their duties. Until now, for failing to act in unison, they have been no more than blind and passive tools in the hands of wicked men, that is kings, nobles, priests, self-seekers, aristocrats, statesmen. . . . The sans-culottes, responsible for providing all the needs of the hive, no longer want to tolerate such sluggish and injurious hornets, proud and parasitic, either above us or among us.

OLD MAN   My brothers, my children, I too am a sans-culotte!

.   .   .

Eventually the former monarchs arrive in chains to begin their isolation from the human race. They are depicted as pretentious fools, vile scoundrels, ferocious animals, and political assassins whose selfish ambitions have cost millions of lives and set nation against nation. They quarrel over who was responsible for the failure to crush the revolution in France. When the pope complains about sharing the island with schismatics Catherine the Great attacks him and forces him to admit that popes and priests are charlatans and thimble-riggers. A general free-for-all breaks out over a piece of black bread which the Spanish king has managed to bring ashore. As the sans-culottes leave the island, the volcano begins to erupt violently. "Good Virgin, help me," pleads the king of Spain; "If I escape I'll become a sans-culotte." "And I will take a wife," cries the pope. "As for me," exclaims Catherine the Great, "I'll join the Jacobin and Cordelier Clubs!" The curtain closes as the earth opens up and engulfs the former monarchs in flames.

The Committee of Public Safety was delighted with the drama. Despite the demands of the war effort, it willingly authorized the twenty pounds of gunpowder needed for a realistic eruption at the end of each performance. In addition it ordered and distributed 6,000 copies of the play. One member of the Jacobin Club wanted the Commune to order the piece performed in all Paris theatres. The play was successfully repeated in Rouen and other provincial centres. And the reviews in the Jacobin press were enthusiastic. In his paper, *Le Père Duchesne*, Hébert lauded the production under the guise of an old merchant showing his wife the sights of Paris. Describing the fiery demise of the toppled monarchs, the merchant concludes, "There is a spectacle fit for republican eyes!"

At the Opera and some of the bigger theatres there were ex-extravagant pageants such as *L'Inauguration de la république française* by Bouquier and Moline which combined elaborate staging with verse, song, dance, marching, and choral effects. The stage swarmed with actors playing deputies, provincial delegates, various officials, market women, and common citizens of all ages. In five acts this "political opera" re-enacted the ceremonies of the great Festival of Unity and Indivisibility at which the Jacobin constitution had been formally accepted the previous August. Like the festival, the spectacle offered a symbolic résumé of the progress of the Revolution. In Act I song and dance around a figure of Regeneration commemorated the capture of the Bastille. In Act II a ballet glorified the market women who had marched out to Versailles. In Act III ritualistic destruction of symbols of royalty before a statue of Liberty on the Place de la Révolution recalled the overthrow of the monarchy. In Act IV a colossal statue of the French People crushing Federalism atop a symbolic Mountain glorified the triumph of the Jacobins and the Paris populace. Then in the final act the president of the Convention proclaimed the Constitution on the Champs de Mars amid general rejoicing. "It is with such works that public spirit will be formed and kept at the height at which it should be sustained," enthused the *Journal de la Montagne*. The Committee of Public Safety ordered this piece performed at the Opéra, the Théâtre des sans-culottes, and the Théâtre Favart and paid for the costly productions. Beginning in March of 1794 the spectacle was presented more than fifty times.

At the same time the Terror witnessed a flood of anti-clerical plays showing drunken popes, debauched cardinals, and deceitful priests. There were also numerous *pièces de circonstance,* plays improvised to celebrate some recent victory or revolutionary achievement. The recapture of Toulon from the English produced a spate of hastily written dramas mixed with patriotic songs. There were comedies based on the difficulty some oldsters had in adapting to the egalitarian practice of using "tu" instead of "vous" in addressing fellow citizens. Other dramas and vaudevilles centred on equality for bastards, the emancipation of Negroes, production of saltpetre for gunpowder, the advantages of the military draft, or the benefits of the new anti-Christian calendar. Programs ordinarily offered one long play with a ballet, two shorter plays, or several brief ones. Theatrical managers often presented an "escape" play such as the popular *Columbine mannequin* with its comic yet touching love plot, but they were usually careful to combine such a play with a topical one portraying revolutionary ideals.

Playhouses as well as the plays were transformed by the new régime. When the renovated Théâtre de la Nation finally reopened in June of 1794 as the Théâtre de l'Egalité it bore the inscription "FOR THE PEOPLE" across its facade. Inside, aristocratic boxes and balconies had given way to one huge sweep of seats extending from pit to ceiling. The stage boxes had been transformed into niches containing statues of Liberty and Equality. Busts of republican heroes and martyrs decorated the foyer and auditorium. The old baroque ceiling, the gilded friezes, the floral garlands, and the pilasters had all been painted red, white, and blue. The curtain, likewise tricoloured, featured a huge image of Equality in the centre. Thus the architecture reflected the democratic aims of the Committee of Public Safety.

In the spring of 1794, at the same time as it struck down the Hébertists and the Dantonists, the revolutionary government tightened its control over the theatre. In March two new municipal censors were appointed who introduced more severe censorship than hitherto. We have seen how that same month the Committee of Public Safety ordered creation of a theatre for the ordinary people in Paris and ordered other municipalities where there were theatres to organize free performances of civic plays. In May the Commission of Public Instruction began its systematic investigation of the repertories of all theatres. Finally in June the Committee of Public Safety voted to take censorship out of the hands of municipal authorities and to make the Commission of Public Instruction exclusively responsible for supervision of the theatre, not only in Paris, but in France as a whole. Direction of the theatre was thus to be highly centralized. All Frenchmen were to watch didactic dramas screened and approved by the revolutionary government.

INDOCTRINATION THROUGH IMAGES

French revolutionaries had been taught by history and recent literature to believe that art could be a potent instrument in their efforts to create a new breed of citizen. Eighteenth-century Frenchmen were naturally aware of the use which the Church and the monarchy had made of painting and sculpture to indoctrinate or impress the public. Also earlier in the century reformers such as Diderot had stressed the capacity of the visual arts to influence human behaviour:

> Let us exhibit pictures of virtues, and they will find imitators. The sort of exhortation which appeals to the heart by means of the senses, aside from its permanence, is more within reach of the common man. The people make better use of their sight than of their understanding. Images preach, preach without ceasing, and do so without wounding our vanity.

Other reformers, art critics, and even royal officials had called for patriotic or moralistic works in place of the boudoir scenes, trivial genre paintings, still-lifes, landscapes, and other compositions devoid of any serious social message which had inundated the Salons. And Mercier, author of an utopian novel entitled *L'An 2440*, had envisaged the use of paintings, sculptures, and engravings to regenerate the masses. The revolutionaries had only to take up this idea of art as propaganda and to employ it for their cause.

Nothing illustrates better the view of the role of art in society prevalent during the Terror than an episode from a little story by Dulaurent entitled *Le bon père*. The children in the story have demonstrated their civic devotion—the daughter has made clothing for her older brother who is in the army, and the younger son has learned the Declaration of the Rights of Man by heart. The father rewards the children by treating them to a visit to the Louvre, the National Library, and the Vaudeville Theatre. At the art gallery the children are impressed with the portraits of Beaurepaire, Lepelletier, and Marat:

> ONE OF THE CHILDREN Daddy, tell us who this man is wearing the uniform of the National Guard and with his arms raised up to heaven.
>
> FATHER My children, that is a free man, that is Beaurepaire. He was in command of a fortification. The enemy attacked it. Some cowards proposed surrendering it. Beaurepaire called on heaven to witness their dishonourable behaviour. He did not wish to survive such a deed and killed himself.
>
> ONE OF THE CHILDREN And who is this man, Daddy, who is stretched out on his bed? He still seems to be bleeding.
>
> FATHER That is the first martyr of liberty. He was killed because he did his duty. His grateful fatherland has reserved a place for him in the temple of great men. He already has a place in the hearts of all good Frenchmen. And over here you see his comrade who shared his labours and his glory, the man who on a crude block from his underground hollow wrote so many useful truths and who was not fully understood until his death. Take a good look: he is the friend of the people. Never seek any other title.
>
> ONE OF THE CHILDREN Daddy, if painting perpetuates the memory and likeness of the men whom we ought to revere, then we ought to cherish the fine arts.
>
> FATHER Certainly, my children, we must cherish and cultivate the arts.

This idea of the utility of art was reiterated on all sides against a minority who argued that as luxury products the arts were a menace to an austere republican morality. Spokesmen for the Committee of Public Safety, deputies in Convention, members of the Jacobin Club, and revolutionary newspapers all defended the usefulness of the fine arts. For example, the *Décade philosophique* felt that it had a duty to correct the notion that the arts were nothing more than pleasant objects which society could do very well without. Actually, the fine arts were of basic importance because they could turn abstract truths into living realities. "Thus the arts must furnish the quickest and surest means of public education," the journal argued, "and doubtless the legislators who organize public education will not neglect them."

The notion that the arts ought to prove their utility by propagating republican lessons was also vigorously supported by the remarkable art jury which the Convention set up to judge a contest among student artists. The painter David, a leading Jacobin and a member of the Convention, told the legislature that fifty ardent republicans from various professions had been selected as jurors so that the arts would not remain in the same old rut where they had been left by despotism. The proceedings of this jury, which met several times in February of 1794, reveal that they were indeed a group of zealots. Dufourny, who chaired the first session, declared that the arts ought to be appraised on a new basis. "Artists are now going to be judged differently than by an academy," he announced; "it is a matter of determining whether the Revolution has given them a distinctive character, whether they are genuinely revolutionary." In evaluating the students' works the jurors all looked more for republican zeal than artistic skill. And when the jury had completed its official business, it transformed itself into the Revolutionary Art Club and sent its suggestions to the Committee of Public Instruction about how the arts could be converted into ideological weapons.

Many artists themselves joined in the chorus demanding propagandistic art. Some artists were inspired by genuine revolutionary zeal which had been intensified by their struggle to destroy the privileges of the old Royal Academy. Others seem mainly to have been anxious to emphasize the possible utility of art in order to obtain government support at a time when the traditional patronage of the court, the aristocracy, and the Church had disappeared. Those who were sincerely pro-Jacobin or who were willing to conform for the moment formed the Popular and Republican Art Association. The members swore devotion to the Republic, fulminated against suspected counter-revolutionary artists, and practised the liturgy of a Jacobin club. One of the best examples of the attitude toward art among this group was the speech by Jacques Lebrun when the members planted a Tree of Liberty near the Louvre:

> How culpable those blasphemous artists would be who would prostitute their talents by offering counter-revolutionary images, who would forget that their most essential characteristic is to be philosophic, that their primary duty is to choose subjects which tend to instruct, to

reform morals, to inspire love of one's country and enthusiasm for liberty.

At the close of his oration all the members present repeated an oath to employ their talents solely for the utility of the Republic. This Association repeatedly appealed to the government to launch projects for republican art.

Revolutionaries believed that images could serve their cause in a variety of ways. First of all, images could keep alive the memory of the great "days" of the Revolution and the victories of the republican armies—the storming of the Bastille on July 14, 1789; the march of the Parisian market women and National Guard to Versailles on October 5, 1789; the storming of the palace on August 10, 1792; the expulsion of the Girondists from the Convention on June 2, 1793; the inauguration of the new republican constitution on August 10, 1793; or the recapture of Toulon from the British on December 19, 1793. Jacobin leaders hoped that by commemorating such events through art they could arouse and sustain revolutionary fervour.

Jacobins also hoped to stimulate emulation by confronting citizens with portrayals of republican heroism. Their conception of heroic virtue was largely shaped by episodes from classical history. For Jacobins the republican hero of antiquity was a moral giant who was willing to sacrifice personal affections for a higher cause. A favourite example of such heroism was Junius Brutus who had ordered his two sons put to death for conspiring to restore the monarchy in Rome. Another striking model of selfless devotion to the state involved a Spartan woman who saw her elder son killed on the battlements during a siege of the city. Instead of lamenting his death, she called for his younger brother to replace him immediately. A canvas by Naigeon depicting this episode at the Salon of 1793 won praise from republican critics. The neo-classical style, austere and melodramatic, developed by David and other artists, was ideally suited for portraying such exalted conduct.

Jacobins wanted examples of similar heroism during the Revolution itself to be transmitted to the public through works of art —Lepelletier, assassinated for demanding the death sentence for Louis XVI; Bara, killed in his early 'teens in the struggle against counter-revolutionaries in the Vendée; or Viala, mortally wounded at thirteen battling royalists near Avignon. A print depicting the last words of Joseph Chalier, engraved by Tassaert as drawn by Caresme, illustrates how republican artists tried to idealize Jacobin heroes. Chalier had established a radical régime in Lyons in May of 1793, but anti-Jacobins had overthrown him and sentenced him to death. The print portrayed the republican martyr in his prison cell, his arm raised, ready to depart with the executioner. "Why are you crying?" read the inscription. "Death is nothing to those whose intentions are upright and whose conscience is always pure . . . Chalier knows how to die in a manner worthy of the cause he has upheld." Presenting their engraving to the Convention, the artists claimed that Chalier had exhibited the constancy of Socrates and the courage of Scaevola.

The most outstanding idealization of a Jacobin hero was David's painting of Marat, slumped lifeless in the bathtub where he had been struck down by Charlotte Corday while soaking to relieve a skin ailment. The rabid journalist was shown lying serene like a dead Christ. Even the ink pot on the table where he had been working on his newspaper had oddly enough not been tipped over in the assassination, and the victim still held the note from Charlotte Corday in his hand. In presenting this republican *pietà* to the Convention, David envisaged the people approaching his canvas. It was as though the picture was speaking to them:

> He is dead, my friend, struck down while giving you his last morsel of bread; he is dead without even leaving enough to have himself buried. Posterity, you will revenge him, you will say to our descendants how rich he might have been, had he not preferred virtue . . .

At the same time revolutionary leaders wanted art to celebrate the less dramatic virtue of everyday life. Some of the genre paintings exhibited at the Louvre in 1793 show how such works could convey a political or moral message. Petit Coupray's painting, entitled "Le Départ pour les frontières" showed two young lads with knapsacks on their backs swearing an oath before their father to defend their country. The father was portrayed thanking heaven for giving him children so full of courage. A disconsolate daughter pointed out to her brother the grief which their departure would cause their mother. An adolescent held one brother's cap and revealed his longing to set off with them. A still younger lad clung to his mother. And an old governess, who had raised the family, was shown marvelling at their devotion. Other artists had depicted seamstresses making gaiters for French soldiers, workers singing patriotic songs as they manufactured weapons, common folk dancing on the former site of the Bastille, or citizens performing some humane or charitable deed.

In addition revolutionary leaders were confident that symbolic signs and figures would help to impress the new Jacobin faith on the masses. The Revolution produced a number of symbols—the Level, token of equality; the Bonnet, indicator of liberty; the Cockade, emblem of the nation; the Pike, weapon of the free man; the Club, instrument of the popular will; the Fasces, sign of revolutionary solidarity; the Oak, mark of rebirth and social virtue; and the Eye, symbol of divinity and watchfulness. Meanwhile a female trinity appeared to replace Venus, the favourite goddess of the aristocracy; there was Liberty, often carrying a broken yoke or a pike capped with a red bonnet; Equality, usually portrayed carrying a level; and Fraternity, habitually carrying fasces. These new goddesses brought in their train a number of other formidable females—Reason, Nature, Truth, Virtue, Probity, Force, or Victory, usually carrying symbols of their attributes. Force, for example, appeared crowned with oak leaves and armed with a club.

Like Christian iconographers, Jacobins sought to use these symbolic signs and figures in allegorical compositions. Little allegorical engravings frequently illustrated republican manuals and catechisms. The frontispiece to a collection of heroic deeds, entitled *Etrennes patriotiques aux armées françaises*, was typical. "War against Tyrants! Peace and Liberty for Peoples!" declared the caption. A huge female figure, holding a pike topped with a red cap of the Revolution, leads a group of soldiers with drawn swords. A tricolour flag waving in the breeze bears the words "Liberty" and "Equality". Another woman, winged like an angel, soars overhead unrolling a banner bearing the war-cry of the "Marseillaise": "Allons, enfants de la patrie". Such allegories could be employed, not only in engravings, but also in paintings and low reliefs.

On a less elevated plain Jacobins intended to exploit caricatures or cartoons as a medium for propaganda. From the summoning of the Estates General onward various factions employed caricatures to further their cause. Boyer de Nimes had even produced the first history of caricatures in the French language, a counter-revolutionary work intended to expose the foul methods which radicals had used to smear and discredit the monarchy. The author lost his head during the Terror, but his work had served to emphasize the potential influence of caricatures. The cartoons of the Terror were seldom works of art, nevertheless they did effectively communicate the passions of the day. Villeneuve, one of the most productive cartoonists, was obsessed with the guillotine. A typical drawing shows one of these dread machines dripping blood. "A warning to plotters", the caption cries. "Traitors look and tremble: it will not cease its activity until you have lost your life." Another scene shows the royal family, all carrying their severed heads under their arms, presenting themselves in Hell.

There is one variety of propaganda which Jacobins did *not* include in their program. Modern régimes on both the left and the right have spawned endless images of such leaders as Stalin, Hitler, Castro, or Mao. The Jacobins did not develop any such cult of the leader. The revolutionary government was controlled by a committee which was never dominated by a single personality. Suspicion that Robespierre aspired to make himself high-priest of the new cult of the Supreme Being helped to bring about his overthrow. Fearing dictatorship by a single person, Jacobins preferred to idealize martyrs rather than live political leaders. Republican textbooks and catechisms sometimes featured galleries of republican heroes and founders of liberty, but they never included Robespierre or his colleagues. When Jacobins were idealized it was as a collective group represented by the holy Mountain.

Jacobins planned to surround the citizen from birth onwards and at all hours of the day with didactic images in every conceivable form. As a child he would find civic messages in storybooks, in republican primers, on classroom walls, and in gymnasia. As an adult he would encounter republican lessons in paintings or engravings in his home, in low reliefs on public buildings, in statues on central squares, in the decorations at his local club, and in embellishments at the theatre. "Great monuments ought to make strong impressions," Dufourny told the jury judging architectural plans by students; "the walls ought to speak; maxims ought to turn our buildings into moral textbooks." The citizen would also come across republican scenes and symbols in books, newspapers, letterheads, ladies' fans, snuffboxes, playing-cards, crockery, and even furniture. Patriotic beds appeared with the posts carved in the shape of fasces or pikes topped with liberty bonnets.

During the Terror, French artists turned out a considerable number of revolutionary paintings, statues, busts, and engravings, but the output fell far short of the desired goal. The Salons in the Louvre were always considered the best single index of the state of the visual arts in France, yet the recent exhibit held in the summer of 1793 had not been very different from those under the Old Régime. Paintings of the great days of the Revolution, republican allegories, and moralistic genre paintings had formed only a small fraction of the works on display. Moreover, no great monuments had yet been produced to replace the toppled statues of Bourbon kings in public squares. Plaster statues left over from the Festival of Unity and Indivisibility on August 10 of 1793 served as stand-ins, but these fragile works, gradually deteriorating under the impact of the weather, were scarcely effective symbols of the new Republic. Consequently, in the spring of 1794 the Committee of Public Safety made a concerted effort to redirect artistic activity and to conscript the fine arts into the service of the Republic.

The projects were various and far-ranging. The Committee of Public Safety announced plans to create a grandiose national park in the centre of Paris decorated with arches, colonnades, statues, and low reliefs, all illustrating revolutionary themes. Sculptors were called upon to compete in designing for the squares of Paris huge monuments commemorating the glorious epochs of the Revolution which had been celebrated at the great Festival of Unity and Indivisibility. They were also to submit designs for a colossal bronze statue of the French People, trampling down fanaticism, royalism, and Federalism, for the western end of the Ile de Paris. Painters were not asked to compete for any specific project, but were to submit themes of their own choice honouring the Revolution. Architects were called on to compete in designing a Temple of Equality for the Champs Elysées, as well as to develop plans for other republican buildings and popular arenas. And early in July Barère announced yet another ambitious plan —the old customs gates surrounding the city were to be converted into monuments commemorating the outstanding victories of French armies.

Barère took a special delight in the idea of turning these tax-collection posts of the farmers-general into symbols of republican successes. He told the cheering Convention:

> In order to ransack passers-by, in order to impose a rapacious inquisition over provisions and commerce, the General Farm turned the gates of the city into haunts of vampires, and no one approached it without trembling before these dens of finance.

> Now citizens must not approach these gateways without rejoicing in popular successes. The farmer, the traveller, or the foreigner coming to Paris must be able to reach it only by passing through victory monuments.

> The despots allied together at Pilnitz to destroy Paris; well, Paris must display proofs of the destruction of despots. They did not want to leave stone on stone; well, we will engrave on those very stones, in ineffaceable letters, in letters of bronze, the victories over tyrants and the dates when successful battles consolidated the republic.

> Paris henceforth will be the city of a *hundred gates*, and each will point to a military triumph or revolutionary development . . .

Meanwhile the Committee of Public Safety disseminated various forms of visual propaganda. Barère asked the Convention to commission an engraving of the young hero Bara to be distributed to all primary schools in the country "in order there to recall ceaselessly to French youth the purest example of love of the Fatherland and filial devotion". The Committee ordered prints celebrating the heroism of Claude Fabre, a representative on mission in the south who had died trying single-handedly to defend a gun battery in a battle with the Spanish. Other artists were subsidized to portray the heroism of Roman patriots and republicans. At the same time, throughout the winter and spring of 1793-4 the Committee purchased 500-1,200 copies each of various cartoons ridiculing the enemies of the Republic. David himself did some cartoons for the revolutionary government. One shows George III, with a turkey-cock leading him by the nose, in command of an army of blockheads.

Efforts to mobilize the fine arts were by no means confined to Paris. In the provinces Jacobin clubs, local authorities, and representatives on mission also commissioned works of art as propaganda. Maignet, who was on mission to Marseilles, granted an artist named Reattu 3,000 *livres* to begin work on a great allegorical painting depicting Liberty carried in triumph by warriors who had vanquished the priests and kings allied against her. Maignet justified the grant on the grounds that it was urgent to propagate republican ideas by every medium available. And in a provincial city such as Nancy the authorities ordered the sculptor Marlet to create a huge statue of Liberty rising out of the debris of royalty, to be placed in the central square. In the local *Journal républicain* the artist advertised miniature plaster reproductions of this statue as well as busts of various republican heroes to decorate the homes of patriots. In the spring of 1794 both the central revolutionary government and its local branches were thus attempting to approach their goal of surrounding citizens from childhood onward with didactic or inspirational images.

We have discussed various media—books, newspapers, plays, and images—which revolutionary leaders sought to mobilize in their efforts to reshape the mass mind. There was, however, another medium—music—which many republicans considered an even more effective means of propagating the new gospel. Through music civic lessons could be conveyed in a persuasive form. In a review of a collection of songs by Thomas Rousseau, the *Journal des hommes libres*, which as we have seen was one of the leading revolutionary journals, asserted that music was probably older than language, certainly older than knowledge. The journal argued that since music derived from nature itself it had a powerful appeal to human beings, particularly the very young. "Few people read, everybody sings," the newspaper observed. "Song is therefore one of the main avenues which must be opened up for public instruction."

We have seen that many eighteenth-century thinkers were confident that men could be led to practise social virtues if moral lessons were constantly associated with pleasant sensations. To many republicans music seemed an ideal medium for exploiting the potential advantages of this associational psychology. The anonymous compiler of the *Nouveau chansonnier patriote*, a little songbook published at Lille at the height of the Terror, believed that songs were especially suited to appeal to Frenchmen whose gaiety led them to turn everything into couplets. Even the more sober-minded neighbours of France would eventually be infected by republican songs. "The taciturn Englishman, the grave Spaniard, the stock-broker Dutchman, the stolid German will one day smile at the sallies of our songs," the editor predicted, "and soon truth . . . will penetrate among these people through the avenues of pleasure."

Confidence that music could serve as a mass educational weapon was further encouraged by historical precedents. Advocates of revolutionary music never tired of pointing out that the Hebrews, the Greeks, and the Romans had employed vocal music to inculcate religious dogma or civic duties. Above all there was the more recent use of music by the Church, an example which became all the more compelling as the Revolution itself turned into a religious movement. As advanced revolutionaries adopted republican catechisms, patriotic prayers, political commandments, civic altars, and other liturgical trappings, it was natural for them to think of using hymns, chants, and canticles to spread the Jacobin gospel. "If the *Credo* sung from infancy inured so many men to believe what they did," argued the *Journal des hommes libres,* "why should truth not seize the means which error has employed with such success?"

Music seemed ideally suited to reach the illiterate or semi-literate populace. A mass audience appeared possible because the song-writers of the Revolution employed a technique familiar to their predecessors of the Old Régime—namely adaptation of new lyrics to well-known tunes. For these song-writers the music was *not* an end in itself, rather it was an effective means of conveying a message. Songs set to traditional airs or recent popular melodies promised rapid diffusion of the authors' work. Revolutionary hymns were sometimes set to the tunes of dances or amorous songs. The music for Boy's "Veillons au salut de l'Empire", for example, came from a gallant serenade in the comic-opera *Renaud d'Ast* staged back in 1787. Some airs were used repeatedly, and even when compositions were accompanied by new music authors generally indicated a familiar tune to which the words could be sung.

Music seemed all the more valuable as an ideological weapon because of the variety of ways in which it could be used. It seemed indispensable for the vast outdoor festivals by which republican leaders hoped to arouse popular enthusiasm. "No republic without national festivals, no national festivals without music," argued the *Journal de Paris* in November, 1793, in proposing establishment of a National Institute to train republican musicians. In addition to their emotional impact songs and hymns seemed essential for festivals for two reasons. Mass singing, backed by wind instruments, could create the volume needed to reach vast throngs gathered in the open air in an age lacking loudspeakers. And through singing these vast crowds could be drawn into the active participation which was considered vital in democratic festivals.

Music could be used in combination with drama to entertain and educate simultaneously. At the peak of the Terror the theatres produced scores of vaudevilles, operas, ballets, and other spectacles in which revolutionary songs played an important role. Hit songs from productions at the Théâtre du Vaudeville and other playhouses were carried out into the streets and ward assemblies of the capital. Theatre audiences often joined in singing patriotic numbers so that actors and onlookers merged into one fraternal group. Later one republican, Mercier de Compiègne, even produced a manual for enacting musical dramas at home. Entitled *Les Concerts républicains*, his book contained a series of little didactic plays, part prose and part song, plus a selection of hymns, odes, and songs. The author explained that his aim was to instruct, but not in a dry or forbidding fashion. Even partying was to have an ideological function.

From time immemorial men had marched to war to the strains of martial music, but for the French revolutionaries this medium was especially important since they were bent on creating citizen-soldiers inspired with revolutionary zeal. The National Institute of Music was created by the revolutionary government in the autumn of 1793, not only to train musicians for the great festivals, but also to supply the various French armies. When Barère introduced in the Convention a bill for the establishment of a new military school, he emphasized how stirring music would prepare young republicans for battle. "The Republic", he declared, "must penetrate the hearts of citizens through all the senses." Little songbooks appeared either designed specifically for soldiers or containing a section of military songs. The editors of *Le Chansonnier de la Montagne* expressed the hope that it would become the psalter of the soldier. Another editor hoped that before battle soldiers would henceforth sing republican songs instead of praying.

Since music was thought to have a special impact on children, revolutionary leaders expected important results from use of republican songs and hymns in primary schools. The periodical collection of heroic exploits which the Convention ordered to be used in all French schools contained a selection of revolutionary songs. So too did many of the republican catechisms and civic primers designed for school children. Germain Lenormand, the principal of public schools at Rouen, composed ten commandments in song, specially designed to instruct young republicans in their social duties. Another writer, Edme Mentelle, apparently hoped that children would sing his versified version of the thirty-five articles of the 1793 Declaration of the Rights of Man.

But most revolutionaries hoped that music would not be limited to use in state festivals, the theatre, the army, or schools. They hoped that republican music would pervade everyday life. Piis, compiler of a collection entitled *Chansons patriotiques*, believed that songs could help to regenerate morals, destroy superstition, and propagate a pure civism. He expressed the hope that his songs, conveyed by familiar tunes, would spread out from the capital into rural communes. Another editor of a similar collection urged Frenchmen to sing patriotic songs everywhere at all hours; ". . . when the evening star informs you of the time for rest, in your homes, in the fields, at work, during meals, by day, by night, everywhere sing, celebrate the triumph of the free man; recount it to your newborn family so that their first utterings will be a solemn tribute to your liberty."

Altogether the French Revolution produced over three thousand political songs, the vast majority pro-revolutionary. The outpouring mounted from about a hundred and twenty-five in 1789 to more than seven hundred in 1794. At the peak of the Terror revolutionary songs were produced at an average rate of two per day. They appeared not only in innumerable songbooks, but also in sheet-music, newspapers, catechisms, almanacs, and programs for various ceremonies. There were stately hymns, lively choruses, victory odes, marching songs, patriotic couplets, and republican rondos. And there was a great variety of themes. Leafing through the song-books of the Year II, one comes across pieces on such diverse subjects as Liberty and Equality, republican martyrs such as Marat and Bara, the new republican calendar, the creation of a female army, marriage as a civic duty, the iniquities of priests, the liberty of colonies, or the benefits of printing.

The "Carmagnole" combined bloodthirsty lines with a gay tune from the south of France. The song appeared sometime in late August or early September of 1792 just after the royal family had been taken off to prison. Throughout the Terror variations of this song were sung in the theatres, political clubs, or around the guillotine. And the tune was used repeatedly for new patriotic lyrics:

> Madam' Veto avait promis (bis)
> De faire égorger tout Paris. (bis)
> Mais son coup a manqué,
> Grâce à nos canonniers.
>
> Refrain:
> Dansons la Carmagnole,
> Vive le son, (bis)
> Dansons la Carmagnole,
> Vive le son du canon!
>
> Monsieur Veto avait promis (bis)
> D'être fidèle à son pays, (bis)
> Mais il y a manqué,
> Ne faisons plus quartier. (Refrain)
>
> Antoinette avait résolu (bis)
> De nous fair' tomber sur le cul, (bis)
> Mais le coup a manqué,
> Elle a le nez cassé. (Refrain)
>
> . . .
>
> Amis, restons toujours unis, (bis)
> Ne craignons pas nos ennemis. (bis)
> S'ils viennent nous attaquer,
> Nous les ferons sauter. (Refrain)
>
> Oui, je suis sans-culotte, moi, (bis)
> En dépit des amis du Roi. (bis)
> Vivent les Marseillois,
> Les Bretons et nos lois. (Refrain)
>
> . . .

Some songs were inspired by unlikely subjects. "Le Maximum" by Ladré, set to a popular air, praised the ceiling on prices imposed by the Convention, attacked rich merchants, lauded the Jacobin "Mountain", and parodied the *Te Deum* of the church-goer. Thanks to the Jacobins, champions of liberty and brother-hood, all Frenchmen were going to eat and drink at a just price instead of being exploited by rapacious beasts:

> Braves Français, consolons-nous,
> A juste prix, nous allons boire,
> Et sur les tigres et les loups,
> Nous remporterons la victoire.
> La vraie justice est nobiscum,
> Calotins, chantez Te Deum,
> Moi, je chante le Maximum
> Que l'on voit en France,
> J'en ris quand j'y pense,
> De la loi, c'est un beau factum
> Que ce bienfaisant Maximum.

> . . .

> Vous, avides négociants
> Qui cherchiez à nous faire battre,
> Et vous, Messieurs les gros marchands,
> Notre loi vous force à rabattre.
> Des magasins, vous entassiez
> Et toujours, vous enrichissiez,
> Mais vous voilà bien attrapés.
> Qu'en voulez-vous dire?
> Vous n'en pouvez rire;
> Il faut suivre le Maximum,
> Ah! de la loi, quel beau factum!

> . . .

> Eh bien, Français, que dirons-nous
> Des hommes de notre Montagne?
> Ne travaillent-ils pas pour tous?
> La justice les accompagne,
> Ils soutiennent l'égalité,
> Ils veulent la fraternité
> En abolissant la cherté,
> Frappant sur le riche,
> Qui trop fort nous triche,
> Peut-on voir un plus beau factum
> Que le bienfaisant Maximum?

Another song entitled "Le Salpêtre républicain", first sung at the Opéra-comique in February of 1794, urged patriots to go into cellars to scrape the walls for the saltpetre needed for gunpowder. More saltpetre was all that was needed to vanquish Pitt and his

English pirates. It was almost as if the spirit of Frenchmen of former centuries, who had loved liberty despite repression, was now emerging from the soil in the form of nitre to help defeat the wicked enemies of the Republic:

Descendons dans nos souterrains,
La liberté nous y convie,
Elle parle, Républicains,
Et c'est la voix de la patrie,
Lavez la terre en un tonneau
En faisant évaporer l'eau;
Bientôt, le nitre va paraître.
Pour visiter Pitt en bateau,
Il ne nous faut que de salpêtre.

.   .   .

C'est dans le sol de nos caveaux
Que gît l'esprit de nos ancêtres,
Ils enterraient, sous leurs tonneaux,
Le noir chagrin d'avoir des maîtres.
Cachant sous l'air de la gaîté
Leur amour pour la liberté,
Ce sentiment n'osait paraître,
Mais dans le sol, il est resté,
Et cet esprit, c'est du salpêtre.

On verra le feu des Français
Fondre la glace germanique;
Tout doit répondre à ses succès:
Vive à jamais la République!
Précurseurs de la liberté,
Des lois et de l'égalité,
Tels partout on doit nous connaître,
Vainqueurs des bons par la bonté,
Et des méchants par le salpêtre.

.   .   .

Year II of the French Republic saw belief in equality at its height. "La Liberté des nègres", by Piis, sung to a well-known tune, rejoiced over the recent abolition of slavery by the Convention. First performed in the Tuileries ward of Paris in February of 1794, the song proclaimed that all men were now brothers sharing the same hereditary rights. "Colour falls, and man remains!", the song-writer concluded:

59

Le saviez-vous, Républicains,
Quel sort était le sort du nègre?
Qu'à son rang, parmi les humains
Un sage décret réintègre;
Il était esclave en naissant,
Puni de mort, pour un seul geste . . .
On vendait jusqu'à son enfant.
Le sucre était teint de son sang,
Daignez m'épargner tout le reste . . . (bis)

De vrais bourreaux, altérés d'or,
Promettant d'alléger ses chaînes,
Faisaient, pour les serrer encor,
Des tentatives inhumaines.
Mais, contre leurs complots pervers,
C'est la nature qui proteste
Et deux peuples, brisant leurs fers,
Ont, malgré la distance des mers,
Fini par s'entendre de reste. (bis)

. . .

Américains, l'égalité
Vous proclame aujourd'hui nos frères.
Vous aviez à la liberté
Les mêmes droits héréditaires.
Vous êtes noirs, mais le bon sens
Repousse un préjugé funeste . . .
Seriez-vous moins intéressants,
Aux yeux des républicains blancs?
La couleur tombe, et l'homme reste! (bis)

. . .

In the late autumn of 1793 the attack on Christianity reached its peak and churches were converted into temples of Reason, Liberty or Equality. François de Neufchâteau's "Hymne à la Liberté" was first sung in November at the ceremony transforming the Church of Saint-Laurent in Paris into such a temple. Later it was used at Tours and a number of other places for similar ceremonies. The hymn depicts Sacred Liberty driving out fanaticism and inaugurating a new religion based on nature and consisting of republican virtue, devotion to the Fatherland, and service to the Sovereign People. Originally sung to the tune "Veillons au salut de l'Empire", it was later set to music composed by Lesueur:

O Liberté, Liberté sainte!
Déesse d'un peuple éclairé!
Règne aujourd'hui dans cette enceinte,
Par toi ce temple est épuré!
Liberté! devant toi, la raison chasse l'imposture;
L'erreur s'enfuit, le fanatisme est abattu,
Notre évangile est la nature,
Et notre culte est la vertu.

. . .

Aimer sa Patrie et ses frères,
Servir le Peuple souverain,
Voilà les sacrés caractères,
Et la foi d'un Républicain.
D'un enfer chimérique
Il ne craint point la vaine flamme;
D'un ciel menteur
Il n'attend point les faux trésors;
Le ciel est dans la paix de l'âme,
Et l'enfer est dans les remords.

. . .

Soutiens contre de vils esclaves
La République et ses enfants.
Notre cause est juste, ils sont braves,
Fais-les revenir triomphants.
Quand par eux des tyrans
La rage impuissante est punie,
Veillons pour eux,
Et que la France, à leur retour,
Leur offre une famille unie
Par la nature et par l'amour.

Use of these songs and hymns appears widespread during the Terror. They were sung in the theatres where many spectacles were musical productions while others mixed prose with song. They were sung in the sectional or ward assemblies where the sans-culottes—that is the small shopkeepers, artisans, and workers —gathered locally to make their will felt. So many singing delegations arrived at the Convention that Danton protested vigorously that it was the function of a legislature to pass laws in prose, not to enter songs in the record book. And we read in a variety of sources of street-singers on the quays and intersections of the capital seeking a few coins in return for topical songs. Apparently the situation was the same in some parts of the provinces. "We sing here too," the president of the Jacobin Club at Chartres wrote in a letter to the *Journal de la Montagne*: "it is a sure way of effectively inculcating republican lessons by rendering their study gay. The Frenchman is like the swan, he sings even when dying. The last words of our heroic volunteers are uttered in song."

Government agencies attempted to stimulate the output of songs and direct their use. In November, 1793, the Committee of Public Safety ordered that the "Marseillaise" was to be sung regularly every *décadi*—the republican substitute for Sunday—at all theatres and whenever the public demanded it. In March the council of the Paris Commune ruled that no songs other than patriotic pieces were to be tolerated in public places. Various government bodies bought and distributed songs of which they approved. On one occasion the Paris Commune ordered 25,000 copies of a patriotic song after hearing it performed. The Commission of Public Instruction ordered publication and distribution of Lebrun's republican ode about the worship of the Supreme Being. And the Committee of Public Safety made repeated appeals to musicians to exploit all the resources of their art in composing songs and hymns calculated to arouse the passions and memories of the Revolution.

The largest government effort to mobilize music got under way in February of 1794. The Committee of Public Safety agreed to a proposal of the musicians of the Paris National Guard that the government subsidize a fifty- to sixty-page periodical to be distributed each month to all 550 districts in France in order to provide music for great national festivals. Each number was to contain at least one symphony, one hymn or chorus, one rondo or quick step, one military march, and one patriotic song. Copies of this periodical were sent to the principal theatres as well as to every district in the country. Then in July the government began to subsidize a second monthly collection, this one to consist of simpler, more popular songs to be used by country folk on the republican Sunday or by the armed forces. The government leased the home of an *émigré* to the publishers to serve as a production centre for these periodicals plus the thousands of copies of sheet music required for state festivals.

In the spring and early summer of 1794 various periodicals lauded these efforts to publish republican music on a wide scale. Early in May the *Décade philosophique* praised the revolutionary government for imitating the legislators of antiquity who had made music one of the basic supports of society and government:

> In the hands of the wisest lawmakers music was one of the most powerful means which they employed to enlighten men, to purify and moderate morals, to mould public opinion, to inspire love of one's country and respect for the laws, to sustain patience, to excite the courage of their warriors, and to nurture in all hearts the seed of useful and generous deeds.

As the Terror reached its crescendo, in the very midst of political crisis, harried by hundreds of urgent problems, the members of the Committee of Public Safety repeatedly turned their attention to music. They dispatched musicians and patriotic songs to various units of the French army. They hired a composer to write works especially for national festivals. They provided for the expenses of the National Institute of Music and gave it a Paris mansion for its headquarters. They made arrangements for popular open-air concerts. And, with a certain sense of irony, they ordered that all the instruments found in *émigré* homes be collected and classified to create a sort of arsenal for republican musicians. Clearly the members of the great Committee felt that music was a vital medium in their effort to create a regenerate France.

In their efforts to mould a novel type of citizen Jacobins hoped to employ not only print, drama, images, and music, but pastimes and festivals as well. "Actually everything ought to have a moral purpose among a republican nation," argued one of the reports of the Popular and Republican Art Association; "the people ought to meet with lessons even in their diversions." The idea of giving pastimes and festivities a political purpose was scarcely new. In his *Considérations sur le gouvernement de la Pologne*, written back in 1772, Rousseau had proposed using children's games, athletic contests, and popular festivals as means of arousing patriotism and inculcating civic virtue. But only with the establishment of the Jacobin revolutionary government in Year II of the French Republic did a modern state attempt to implement this idea on a vast scale.

Children would find republican lessons in their amusements. Toy guillotines appeared and building-block models of the Bastille which the child could demolish with toy cannon. As little boys played on the street with wooden guns or swords they could learn to defend their country against enemies on the frontiers or counter-revolutionaries within. And a song by Piis taught children to draw political lessons from seemingly neutral games. A house of cards could remind them of the châteaux in the countryside swept away by the breath of liberty. A kite flying high could suggest the Frenchman enjoying his rights in a new age. A seesaw could become an object lesson in good government where merit alternated in power. Ninepins could illustrate the inevitable fate of the coalition aligned against France. Every game could convey some such moral—even blowing bubbles could suggest anti-republican plots which might look attractive for a moment only to evaporate when exposed to the air.

Adults too were to find lessons in their diversions. We have already seen that if they went to the theatre they would find that even ballets, vaudevilles, and comedies had been given an ideological purpose. We have seen too that under the Republic amorous themes were to yield to revolutionary or moral subjects in the songs of the people. Dancing was likewise to serve a patriotic purpose. The aristocratic minuet gave way to the *carmagnole* and other simple but lively democratic dances joined with republican lyrics. And if the citizen sat down with his friends for a game of cards, once again he would be reminded that he lived under a new régime. There was no place for kings, queens, or knaves in the Jacobin republic. Cards were now decorated with figures of Liberty, Equality, Fraternity, Virtue, or some other republican goddess.

But above all it was popular festivals which Jacobin leaders hoped to use to arouse and sustain revolutionary fervour. Popular gatherings had sprung up spontaneously at the very beginning of the Revolution during the Great Fear when a terrible danger had seemed to threaten the land. Neighbouring towns and villages had sent representatives who pledged each other mutual aid. Gradually these gatherings had evolved into provincial and interprovincial festivals. At these *fêtes* patriotic oaths had been repeated, mass had been celebrated, and the banners of the new National Guard had been blessed. Soon revolutionary leaders had realized the advantages of directing such ceremonies for their own purposes. The National Assembly had organized a great national Festival of Federation on the Champ de Mars on July 14, 1790, the first anniversary of the capture of the Bastille.

The people streamed out from the city to transform the Champ de Mars into a vast amphitheatre. Young and old, rich and poor, gaily dressed women and black-clad priests all joined in picking and shovelling. Despite torrents of rain on the day of the festival, the event was highly successful. Representatives of all the new departments had paraded on to the field, the banners of the National Guard had been blessed, Talleyrand had celebrated mass on the altar of the Fatherland, and Lafayette had administered an oath to the assembled throng "to be faithful forever to the nation, the law, and the king". Then Louis XVI had sworn to uphold the Constitution. "Today we have a Fatherland and our liberty is assured", one of the delegates from the departments had written, and most of the participants had shared his enthusiasm. Soon monarchy and the church had ceased to provide a rallying-point for Frenchmen, but this festival had revealed what a potent instrument such celebrations could be.

Gradually the nation had become the central object of devotion and the celebrations had taken on an increasingly pagan tone. The triumphal translation of the remains of Voltaire to the Pantheon in July, 1791, planned by Jacques-Louis David, had been a completely lay celebration and had served as a rallying-point for anti-royalists. In 1792 during the last months of the monarchy, the competing factions had each staged festivals in order to arouse support. In April the radicals put on an impressive Festival of Liberty, arranged by David and marked by mass participation. In June the constitutional monarchists had countered with a Festival of Law which had a strong militaristic flavour. Following establishment of the Republic, the Jacobins had made repeated use of festivals or processions to further their cause. David had turned the funerals of the heroes Lepelletier and Lazowski in January and April of 1793 into Jacobin rallies. Then, following the triumph of the Jacobins, David had organized the impressive funeral of Marat in July and the great Festival of Unity and Indivisibility in August. During the Terror the painter was made virtual dictator of the arts, charged with planning public funerals, triumphal processions, and national festivals.

Revolutionary leaders were especially confident of the power of festivals because in them all the arts could be combined to impress the senses and arouse emotion. This was the point made by Marie-Joseph Chénier in a speech to the Convention on public education in November, 1793. Declaring that national festivals ought to play a central role in public education, he continued:

Liberty will be the very soul of our public festivals: they will exist only for her and by her. All the arts, enlarged and sanctified by her, will unite to arouse love for her—architecture raising a temple to her, painting and sculpture vying with each other to portray her image, oratory celebrating her heroes, poetry singing their praises, music rendering hearts submissive to her by lofty and moving harmony, dancing enlivening her triumphs, hymns, ceremonies, symbols, all varied according to the different festivals, but always inspired by her spirit, all ages kneeling before her statue. Such are the materials available to legislators when they discuss how to organize popular festivals: such are the elements to which the Convention must give movement and life.

Above all, the festival seemed to provide an ideal means for creating the kind of mass will which Jacobins thought must prevail in a democratic republic. We have seen that they believed that the sovereign people, like an individual writ large, had to be animated by *une volonté unique*. It was not enough to have informed or enlightened citizens if they did not share common emotions or aspirations. There had to be communion of citizen with citizen. This was precisely what the festival might achieve. Its aim was to get the individual involved. Unlike many of the pageants and parades of the Old Régime, the revolutionary *fête* in its fully developed form was not just something to look at, but something to participate in. The festival could draw citizens into a massive shared experience in which they would march together, swear oaths together, sing together, dance together, emote together. The festival could thus make citizens feel a mystic identity with the general will.

The parade continued to form an essential part of the festival, but now all ages and classes were to take part. In the Festival of Unity and Indivisibility, at which the Jacobin constitution was accepted, the procession was headed by the popular societies, carrying a banner portraying the Eye of Vigilance penetrating a thick cloud. Then came the Convention, eight of whose members carried an ark displaying tablets inscribed with the rights of man and the constitution. The Convention was surrounded by delegates from the eighty-seven departments of France, all linked together by a tri-coloured cordon. A mass of the ordinary citizens of Paris formed the central corps of the parade. Next followed a military group, escorting in triumph a float drawn by eight white horses and carrying an urn filled with the ashes of heroes who had died for their country. A detachment of infantry and cavalry, accompanying cartloads of debris of the symbols of monarchy and aristocracy, brought up the rear of the long procession.

In his plan for this great Festival of Unity and Indivisibility, David emphasized the participation in the parade of all members of society massed together indiscriminately, although characterized by their distinctive marks:

> Thus shall one see the president of the provisional executive council abreast with the blacksmith; the mayor with his scarf side by side with the wood-chopper or mason; the judge, in his robes and his plumed hat, next to the dyer or shoemaker. The black African, differing only in colour, shall walk beside the white European. The interesting scholars of the institution for the blind, drawn on a moving platform, shall present the touching spectacle of misfortune honoured. You, too, shall be there, tender nurslings of the foundling asylum, carried in white bassinettes: you shall begin to enjoy your civil rights which you have so justly recovered. And you, worthy labourers, you shall carry in triumph the useful and honourable tools of your calling. Finally, in the midst of this numerous and industrious family, one will especially notice a truly triumphal car formed by a simple plough on which will be seated an old man and his aged wife, pulled by their own children —a touching example of filial devotion and veneration of old age.

Statues, signs, and symbols were employed to heighten the visual impact of the *fête*. In the Festival of Unity and Indivisibility the procession halted at five sites, all decorated with huge plaster monuments which served as focal points for imposing rites and observances. These stopping-places provided republican substitutes for the traditional stations of the cross. At the site of the Bastille there was a colossal goddess of Nature pressing waters of regeneration from her ample breasts. On the Boulevard Poissonnière there was a large triumphal arch commemorating the march of the market-women to Versailles back in October, 1789. On what was now the Place de la Révolution, atop the pedestal where a statue of Louis XV had once stood, there appeared a colossal statue of Liberty. At the Place des Invalides there stood a gigantic figure of the French people annihilating Federalism. And on the Champ de Mars at the fifth and last station there was an altar of the Fatherland where the constitution was proclaimed and the people swore to defend it to the death. Besides these monuments, there were many other features calculated to appeal to the eye—fasces symbolizing unity, tricoloured ribbons, liberty caps, and garlands of flowers.

The most impressive symbol employed in a popular festival during the Terror was the Mountain erected on the Champ de Mars—now called the Champ de Réunion—for the Festival of the Supreme Being in June, 1794. "La Montagne", as we have observed, was the nickname of the Jacobins who were now guiding the Revolution. On the spot where a civic altar had stood since the Festival of Federation back in 1790, organizers of the *fête* had built a huge artificial Mountain complete with boulders, caves, trees, and bushes. On the peak a Liberty Tree stood silhouetted against the sky and smoke curled up from incense burning in giant braziers. The Mountain was large enough to hold the members of the Convention on the summit, a huge corps of musicians and singers lower down, and on the sides a vast choir representing the Paris sections. This immense symbol served as the focal point for the imposing ceremonies which marked the climax of the procession through the streets of Paris.

Oratory played an important part in most revolutionary festivals. In the Festival of the Supreme Being, Robespierre preached a sermon in two parts at the Tuileries Garden. He managed to depict the Almighty as a republican supporter, sponsor of the Jacobin world mission, and author of the rights of man:

> Republican Frenchmen, that happiest of days has finally arrived which the French people dedicate to the Supreme Being. Never has the world which he created offered him a spectacle more worthy of his attention. He has seen tyranny, crime, and imposture ascendant on earth; at this moment he sees an entire nation, at grips with the oppressors of the human race, suspend the pursuit of its heroic labours in order to raise up its thoughts and votive offerings to that great Being who gave it the mission to undertake these tasks and the strength to carry them out.

> Was it not he whose immortal hand wrote the death sentence of tyrants in the human heart by inscribing there the code of justice and equality? Was it not he who decreed the establishment of the Republic since the beginning of time, and made liberty, good faith and justice the order of the day for all times and all peoples?

The Incorruptible then went on to remind Frenchmen that they could best honour the Divinity by living virtuously, by purifying the earth, and by annihilating tyrants.

When Robespierre had completed the first part of his oration, and the crowd had sung a hymn, he descended from the platform and ignited a cardboard statue of Atheism which went up in flames to disclose a smoke-stained image of Wisdom underneath. Robespierre then gave the second part of his address before the procession moved off to the Champ de Réunion. Republican homilies, eulogies of revolutionary martyrs, and panegyrics about French victories were common features of festivals in Paris and the provinces. Such orations were difficult for large crowds to hear in an age before loudspeakers, but evidently they were considered indispensable. The best speeches were reprinted in little manuals so that they could be re-used in local ceremonies every *décadi* or republican Sunday. Speech was turned into print in order to be brought alive again in the remote villages of France. There in small local festivals speech was probably a fairly effective medium of communication.

But it was music which dominated the Festival of the Supreme Being. Not only did musical corps play appropriate patriotic selections at various stages, but the people joined in mass singing at two high-points in the ceremonies. The musicians of the National Institute of Music had carefully prepared the people for their rôle. Two days before the festival they had assembled school children from each ward to teach them the words and music of hymns composed for the festival. Then on the very eve of the *fête* musicians from the Institute, carrying their instruments and accompanied by student assistants, had gone out in twos or threes to every ward to teach adults the same pieces. Meanwhile the printers had worked through the night producing copies of the hymns for mass distribution. At the Tuileries Garden, between the two parts of Robespierre's discourse, the people joined in singing a hymn to the Supreme Being by Désorgues with music by Gossec:

I

Père de l'Univers, suprême intelligence,
Bienfaiteur ignoré des aveugles mortels,
Tu révélas ton être à la reconnaissance
Qui seul éleva tes autels.

II

Ton temple est sur les monts, dans les airs, sur les ondes
Tu n'as point de passé, tu n'as point d'avenir:
Et sans les occuper, tu remplis tous les mondes
Qui ne peuvent te contenir.

At the ceremonies on the Champ de Réunion mass singing reached its climax. An immense corps of professional musicians and singers occupied the upper slopes of the artificial Mountain. Below them ranged 2,400 choristers made up of ten old men, ten mothers, ten girls, ten young men, and ten little boys from each of the forty-eight wards of Paris. The men and boys sat on one side, the women and girls on the other. On the surrounding field the rest of the procession likewise massed in groups according to sex. From atop a tall column near the Mountain, musicians used a tricoloured banner and trumpets to direct this vast choir in singing another hymn, this time by Chénier to the stirring tune of the "Marseillaise". An oath to annihilate crime and tyranny formed the refrain. The first verse was sung by all the men on the Mountain, with all the males in the crowd joining in the refrain. Then all the mothers and girls on the Mountain sang the second verse, with all the females in the crowd echoing the refrain. Finally the whole choir united for the last verse, with the whole crowd responding. Obviously the aim was to achieve as great involvement of the people as possible.

Print too played its part in these popular festivals. Printed slogans appeared on banners, floats, tablets, pedestals, and obelisks. In January of 1794 the little commune of Ferté-sur-Marne staged a festival in honour of the republican soldiers who had recently recaptured Toulon from the British. The procession, which included floats, republican goddesses, vestal virgins, common people, and contingents of local Jacobins, ended up in a field where a symbolic Mountain had been erected. At the foot of this Mountain stood a large obelisk bearing these inscriptions:

- REASON AND FORCE HAVE FOUNDED THE REPUBLIC
- HONOUR TO THE GENIUSES WHO HAVE AROUSED LOVE OF LIBERTY
- HONOUR TO THE SANS-CULOTTES WHO HAVE DEFENDED IT
- NOBLES AND PRIESTS NO LONGER EXIST
- THE PEOPLE ARE ETERNAL
- THE FORCE OF REASON AND THE FORCE OF THE PEOPLE ARE IDENTICAL

This same provincial celebration at Ferté-sur-Marne illustrates the symbolic rites, pantomimes, and several other common elements in Jacobin *fêtes*. En route to the holy Mountain the procession halted in the market square at the foot of a Liberty Tree where a young girl representing Liberty set fire to relics of royalism, feudalism, and fanaticism. Next she broke the chains binding a group of children dressed in dirty, tattered clothes. The goddess then presented the children with simple but clean attire and conducted them on to her chariot. The festival concluded with a fraternal banquet and popular dancing. Other festivals included busts of classical heroes, mock battles, little theatrical productions, and salvos of gunfire. The festival thus brought together every available medium to form an adaptable propaganda weapon and an instrument for social control.

In May, 1794, the Convention approved an ambitious plan for national festivals introduced by Robespierre on behalf of the Committee of Public Safety. The festival of the Supreme Being, which was to launch the program, was intended to make religion, hitherto a devisive factor in the Revolution, into a force for unity. Robespierre believed that upright men could agree on two simple dogmas—the existence of the divinity and the immortality of the soul. The prospect of reward or punishment in the hereafter would provide underpinning for republican morality. In addition to this inaugural festival, there were to be annual celebrations of the capture of the Bastille, the overthrow of the monarchy, the execution of Louis XVI, and the triumph of the Jacobins over the Girondists. And every tenth day, on the republican Sunday, there would be lesser ceremonies in honour of the Deity and nature, martyrs of liberty, love of the Fatherland, hatred of tyrants, and various other social virtues. This cycle of four annual festivals and thirty-six *fêtes décadaires* would replace the holy days of the old Christian calendar. In Paris, in provincial centres, and in small villages Frenchmen would unite in periodic rituals aimed at creating like-minded and dedicated citizens from one end of the country to the other.

The various ingredients of the revolutionary *fête* illustrate the interplay of tradition and innovation in the French Revolution. Folk dancing, symbolic trees, and popular festivities all went back, like the maypole, to a very old Europe. Bundles of fasces, triumphal arches, vestal virgins, and Plutarchian heroes were borrowed from classical antiquity. Republican stations, civic altars, communal feasts, busts of martyrs, periodic holy days, and many other features sprang from Catholic traditions. Still other elements of Jacobin rites and ceremonies probably had Protestant origins—mass singing of hymns, responsive reading of sacred texts, and interminable sermons. But despite all these traditional elements, Jacobin festivals embodied certain novel features which gave them a modern flavour. Mass participation, the assault on all the senses, and manipulation by the state suggest in retrospect the demonstrations of modern totalitarian states on both the left and the right.

Every state attempts to attach citizens to its form of government through such means as patriotic anthems, oaths to the flag, commemorative holidays, or the teaching of national history. A revolutionary government faces in an acute form this problem of engendering mass allegiance since it must persuade citizens to support a new set of values and institutions. In France by the spring of 1794 the Jacobin program of indoctrination was reaching its peak. The government was tightening its grip on the press, preparing closer control over the theatre, beginning to distribute revolutionary music, launching an ambitious art contest, and initiating a great cycle of popular festivals. On April 20 during a long speech to the Convention outlining the objectives of the revolutionary government, Billaud-Varenne made it clear that one basic aim was to employ every available medium in order to create a novel kind of Frenchman wedded to the Jacobin constitution:

> To forget, in a free state, to enlighten the nation by all the means which appeal to the senses and the heart is to lose sight of that which can contribute most effectively to reform; it is to endanger liberty by neglecting to create a national character which more and more identifies the people with its constitution.

But just as the Jacobin propaganda campaign was reaching full development the revolutionary government began to disintegrate. Inside the Committee of Public Safety the old spirit of co-operation gradually broke down. Collot d'Herbois and Billaud-Varenne considered Robespierre a laggard. Robespierre's associate, Saint-Just, accused Carnot of aristocratic connections and quarrelled with him over military policy. Carnot countered by accusing Robespierre and Saint-Just of trying to become dictators. When criticized Robespierre withdrew, making him appear irresponsible and raising suspicions that he was intriguing against his colleagues. The Robespierrists also had alienated many members of the Committee of General Security, the police committee of the revolutionary government, by setting up a police bureau of their own and failing to consult their colleagues when drafting the law of 22 Prairial, an important new law reorganizing the Revolutionary Tribunal and redefining counter-revolutionary activity. Once the revolutionary government became divided, it became vulnerable because its power was never absolute: the Convention could always withdraw its mandate.

Meanwhile the Robespierrists had lost support in the Convention and on the streets. The law of 22 Prairial alarmed many deputies because the slightest criticism of the government could lead to the guillotine. Many Conventionnels such as Barras, Carrier, Fouché, Fréron, or Tallien knew that Robespierre disapproved of their radical de-Christianizing activities, their bloodthirsty suppressions in the provinces, or their shady financial transactions. Fear for their lives made it possible for extremists and moderates to unite against Robespierre and his associates. The fact that French armies had pushed the enemy across the frontiers and had stamped out most counter-revolutionary activity inside the country made it seem safe for the Convention to assert itself once again. At the same time the Robespierrists had alienated the popular forces in the capital by purging extremist leaders such as Hébert and by trying to hold down wages. When the Convention ordered the arrest of Robespierre and his friends on 9 Thermidor (July 27) the Parisian sans-culottes did not rally effectively to their aid.

Some of those who struck down the Robespierrists thought that they were carrying the Revolution forward or would be able to use the terrorist machinery for their own purposes. To their surprise 9 Thermidor opened the way for a mounting revulsion against the Terror and for dismantling of the revolutionary government. The Committee of Public Safety was transformed from a self-perpetuating oligarchy and master of the

Convention into one of several committees subservient to the legislature. The Revolutionary Tribunal was drastically reformed and set about trying notorious terrorists. The Jacobin clubs were first forbidden to correspond with each other before being closed altogether in November. Meanwhile the dreaded Paris Commune disappeared, the power of the turbulent sections or wards was reduced, and the National Guard was reorganized so as to exclude poorer citizens. The purged National Guard and the regular army were then used to crush the sans-culottes when they rose twice in the spring of 1795 demanding cheap bread and the Jacobin constitution. Following these abortive insurrections in Paris the last members of the great revolutionary committees were deported and a White Terror swept many regions.

As the revolutionary government was dismantled the whole social and moral climate shifted. At the peak of the Terror simplicity of dress and moral austerity had been the order of the day. Now the *jeunesse dorée*—the gilded youth—with their brilliant and ostentatious attire, ruled the streets where recently the sans-culottes had held sway. Ladies who had been forced to abandon ribbons and lace during the reign of the Jacobins now happily turned to all sorts of eccentricities of dress. In Clairville's play *Arlequin perruquier* the hero rejoices with his mistress Columbine that fashion has come back again:

> Since the ninth of Thermidor
> Brought joyous liberty,
> The golden things appear once more—
> Our jewels and finery!

Theatres, cafés, and ballrooms flourished. The goddess of the day, the beautiful Mme. Tallien, known as Our Lady of Thermidor, appeared on occasion dressed as Diana, bust half-bare and clad—if one may use that word—in a tunic which did not come below her knees. Thus Robespierre's Republic of Virtue gave way to the republic of easy virtue.

In this new social milieu the Jacobin cultural program collapsed. Print ceased to serve as a means for creating like-minded citizens from one end of France to another. During the Terror the Convention had legislated for a compulsory primary school system in which the Declaration of Rights, the Constitution of 1793, and tales of republican heroism were to have been basic texts, but that scheme was replaced by one which abandoned extreme democratic principles. The textbook contest launched by the Convention was not judged until more than fifteen months after the downfall of Robespierre when the whole political climate had shifted. And as the machinery of the Terror was dismantled, books, pamphlets, and newspapers once again voiced a bewildering variety of conflicting views. Some democratic papers such as the *Journal des hommes libres* continued publication, but they were outnumbered by reactionary sheets such as the *Orateur du peuple* or the *Ami des citoyens*. Some papers like the *Nouvelles politiques* openly wished for an early return of the monarchy. Under the new conservative Directory established in 1795 most papers assailed the régime from the left or the right.

The theatre revealed the same bitter divisions among Frenchmen in the wake of the Terror. Revolutionary dramas were hooted from the stage, patriotic symbols were torn from the walls, busts of Marat and other martyrs were smashed, and actors who had supported the Jacobins were greeted with hisses and insults. When radicals opposed such demonstrations bloody riots broke out in many theatres. In the spring of 1795 there was a spate of anti-Jacobin plays. In Tissot's play, entitled *On respire,* the terrorist Volmar, who is in love with Lucille Dercourt, threatens to kill her father if she does not marry him. Lucille, who loves Dorval, is about to sacrifice herself, when Volmar is arrested for plotting against the representatives of the people. Dorval exclaims:

> Friends, let us swear eternal war against all terrorists. Let us not be deceived by these chameleons. Let us not spare them. They have oppressed us enough. Let us swear to hunt them down into the deepest hideouts!
> EVERYBODY   We so swear!

To avoid disturbances and to cater to a growing weariness of propaganda, theatres turned increasingly to non-political dramas.

But even neutral plays represented frustration of Jacobin plans for theatre as a school for civism.

Instead of all singing in unison as the Jacobins intended, Frenchmen divided into warring camps each chanting its battle songs. Anti-Jacobins often greeted the "Marseillaise" and "Ça ira" with boos and catcalls, and sought to impose their song, the "Reveil du peuple", on performers and audiences alike. This song attacked Jacobins as scoundrels, despots, and drinkers of blood:

> Peuple français, peuple de frères,
> Peux-tu voir sans frémir d'horreur
> Le crime arborer les bannières
> Du carnage et de la terreur?
> Tu souffres qu'une horde atroce
> Et d'assassins, et de brigands.
> Souille par son souffle féroce
> Le territoire des vivants.
>
> Quelle est cette lenteur barbare?
> Hâte-toi, peuple souverain,
> De rendre aux monstres du Thénare
> Tous ces buveurs de sang humain!
> Guerre à tous les agents du crime!
> Poursuivons-les jusqu'au trépas!
> Partage l'horreur qui m'anime!
> Ils ne nous échapperont pas!
>
> Ah! qu'ils périssent, ces infâmes
> Et ces égorgeurs dévorants,
> Qui portent au fond de leur âmes
> Le crime et l'amour des tyrans!
> Mânes plaintifs de l'innocence
> Apaissez-vous dans vos tombeaux,
> Le jour tardif de la vengeance
> Fait enfin pâlir vos bourreaux.

Some song-writers who had recently been lauding Jacobins adapted to the changing market by celebrating the downfall of Robespierre. When the new Directory ordered patriotic songs sung at theatres, some of the audiences left the hall or blew their noses loudly during numbers of which they disapproved. Sometimes performers provoked incidents by singing patriotic pieces with very bad grace or by playing them before tuning their instruments.

The visual arts also illustrate the breakdown of the Jacobin program. More than a year after execution of Robespierre an art

jury announced its judgment of the large number of works submitted in response to the contests announced by the Committee
of Public Safety. Some models for the huge monuments intended
for the squares of Paris were praised, but the monuments themselves were judged inappropriate or too expensive to erect. Most
of the painters who won encouragements for revolutionary
sketches subsequently switched to traditional—and safer—themes.
Political subjects formed only a small fraction of the exhibition
in the Louvre in 1795, and several of these portrayed victims
of the Terror or anti-Jacobin allegories. Meanwhile the market
for Jacobin engravings and busts had collapsed. In a little play
by Gouffré entitled *Arlequin sculpteur* the hero pokes fun at his
neighbour Gilles who is going bankrupt doing images of Jacobin
heroes:

> Now that true freedom has been won
> Your ugly business cannot thrive.
> The wrathful portraits you have done
> Can only serve to keep alive
> The memory of brothers' deaths.

The Jacobin idea of a cycle of republican festivals was not
abandoned, but the program lost much of its momentum. The
festival planned to honour the teenage heroes Bara and Viala
scheduled for 10 Thermidor was never held. David who had
planned the impressive *fêtes* of the preceding years was arrested
and was lucky to escape with his life. Once David ceased to be
pageant-master of the Republic, state festivals no longer were
staged on such a massive scale or marked by such broad popular
participation as the festivals of Unity and Indivisibility or of the
Supreme Being. Official ceremonies often consisted of a concert
given in the chamber of the legislature rather than great outdoor
celebrations. The anniversary of the execution of Louis XVI—
an occasion the Jacobins had planned to make a grand national
holiday—was commemorated on January 21, 1795, on a very
modest scale. A mere hundred copies of the "Chant du départ"
furnished the necessary music. And under the Directory state

Arlequin sculpteur quotation from *The Theatre of the French Revolution*,
by Marvin Carlson. Copyright © 1966 by Cornell University. Used by
permission of Cornell University Press.

ceremonies honoured the memory of Girondist martyrs and celebrated the overthrow of Robespierre.

The Thermidorian reaction thus cut short or rendered abortive the ambitious propaganda projects of the revolutionary government. The short duration of the Jacobin dictatorship was the fundamental reason for the failure of the first modern effort to educate a new citizenry through mass indoctrination. The Jacobins did not achieve power until early June of 1793 and did not institute their *gouvernement révolutionnaire* until October. That dictatorial régime lasted only ten months before Robespierre was overthrown and reaction set in. Moreover the propaganda efforts of this dictatorial régime had only begun to take full shape in the final few months before 9 Thermidor. By contrast the Bolsheviks have had fifty years, and the Chinese Communists eighteen, in which to attempt to create a new Soviet man or novel Chinese citizen. And even these régimes have scarcely succeeded in regenerating human nature.

The Jacobin program suffered from other serious weaknesses besides lack of time. To begin with they were far too confident of their capacity to create a new breed of citizens. We have seen that this optimism sprang from their belief that the mind of the child was almost completely malleable, especially at a very early age. However the bulk of the population was not made up of children, but of adults whose motives and habits had been shaped by the Old Régime. Plato had seen the dilemma in his *Republic* where Socrates explained that to found the ideal state the philosopher kings would have to begin by sending out into the country all inhabitants who were more than ten years old in order that, unaffected by the practices of their parents, children could be trained in new habits and laws. The French revolutionaries had no way of sending adults away so that they could start afresh with unspoiled youths. The very psychological assumptions which made the revolutionaries optimistic about the possibility of permanently shaping children's minds ought to have made them pessimistic about the likelihood of regenerating older citizens. Yet the immediate fate of the Republic depended on adults.

Moreover the Jacobin program of indoctrination was handicapped by the limitations of existing media in a pre-electronic age. The major mass medium available in the late eighteenth century was still the printing press, but its power was limited by the high rate of illiteracy in France. In many areas more than half the population was not literate enough even to sign the marriage register. Printed propaganda could of course be read aloud in cafés, political clubs, civic festivals, and classrooms (where they were in operation), but this only partially offset the limitations of illiteracy. Many forms of printed propaganda—patriotic almanacs, republican thoughts for each day, little histories of republics past and present—were primarily designed for use in the home. We have seen that many revolutionaries hoped that music could convey lessons to the illiterate masses, but propagandists still had to rely largely on newspapers, almanacs, or song-books to spread new lyrics. Public plays might have reached the unlettered, but theatres and actors were available only in larger urban centres. Eighty-five per cent of the population was rural.

At the same time Jacobins never really grasped the scale of operations which their theories of mass indoctrination logically involved. Rarely did they comprehend the staggering problems involved in reaching 26,000,000 Frenchmen with the same messages. While praising the monthly collections of festival music subsidized by the Committee of Public Safety, the *Journal des théâtres* pictured all Frenchmen singing the same song every republican Sunday under the shade of a single symbolic Liberty Tree, but the journal did not explain how the 550 copies—one for each district—were going to provide hymn-books for such a vast choir. There was no guarantee that the district authorities would run off additional copies locally. The government did print 400,000 copies of the Constitution and the Declaration of the Rights of Man, and 150,000 copies of the collection of heroic deeds, but usually the number of copies of printed propaganda was much more limited. The government purchased from six hundred to five thousand copies of each newspaper which it subsidized, but most of these copies went to the army rather than to popular societies in the departments. The total of about three thousand copies destined for the departments did not even provide one copy for each of the five to eight thousand Jacobin clubs spread throughout France. The number of engravings purchased was even smaller—usually about one thousand—yet there were more than forty thousand municipalities. Only further research will enable us to determine how far these deficiencies were off-set by local efforts.

Even if Jacobins had comprehended the massive quantities of propaganda needed to indoctrinate the most populous nation in Europe, it is doubtful whether they could have found the necessary money and materials at a time when they were waging war against a foreign coalition. Consequently the Jacobin leaders depended largely on republican works produced privately for sale, guiding this production by censorship, exhortation, and occasional encouragements. But such propaganda suffered from two serious shortcomings: only those already sympathetic tended to purchase such Jacobin publications; and the price often placed these works beyond easy reach of the labouring class and the peasants who formed the bulk of the population. A first-class carpenter in Paris earned about six *livres* per day at the peak of the Terror and an unskilled worker much less. Advertisements reveal that a newspaper such as the *Journal de la Montagne* cost 50 *livres* per year; a small bust of a republican hero by Marlet cost ten *livres;* an engraving of the martyrdom of Marat by Brion cost twelve *livres* in colour or six in black and white; a little portrait of Bara by Garnerey cost four *livres;* an illustrated songbook such as the *Nouveau Chansonnier patriotique* cost one *livre* fifteen *sous;* and a little republican manual like the *Alphabet républicain* cost one *livre.* Mailing charges made these prices even more prohibitive for a provincial worker or peasant.

Although in the spring of 1794 the revolutionary government was moving toward that central control which we associate with modern propaganda, it never made one member of the government or one agency responsible for directing all indoctrination. At the centre the Committee of Public Safety, the Commission of Public Instruction (an executive body), the Committee of Public Instruction (a legislative organ), the Jacobin Club, and the Paris Commune all shared in initiating and directing propaganda, producing such confusion that some historians have habitually ascribed certain activities to the wrong agencies. As a result of the government's lack of unified planning and its reliance on subsidies rather than direct controls, it sometimes supported propaganda which did not entirely serve its purposes. Such papers as the *Journal des hommes libres,* the *Journal universel,* and the *Anti-fédéraliste* were often more extreme than the Committee of Public Safety as a group. The Committee subsidized the vulgar and blood-thirsty *Père Duchesne* and then guillotined its editor.

The Jacobin program suffered from various other shortcomings. At the lower levels cumbersome administrative machinery and slow communications further impeded efficiency. Also Jacobin propaganda was sometimes curiously aimed at deputies or staunch republicans rather than the general public. The government sent its engravings of the heroism of Fabre to other members of the Convention, apparently in the belief that they needed this inspiration most of all. And the government restricted attendance at the Théâtre du peuple to those who could prove that they were already good citizens, although the aim of revolutionary dramas was to create as well as to sustain patriotism. Often too Jacobin propaganda was overly intellectual and complex. Some allegorical engravings needed long captions to make them intelligible, and even in the great festivals many of the classical allusions and symbols must have been mysterious to the unlettered.

Above all, Jacobin propaganda suffered from the contrast between the heavenly city which it promised and the harsh realities of daily life under revolutionary government. In his great speech to the Convention on February 5, 1794, Robespierre described the visionary republic which the government was attempting to establish:

> We wish an order of things where all base and cruel passions are restrained by the laws, all beneficent and generous feelings aroused; where ambition is the desire to merit glory and to serve one's country; where distinctions are born only of equality itself; where the citizen is subject to the magistrate, the magistrate to the people, the people to justice; where the nation guarantees the welfare of each individual, and each individual proudly shares the prosperity and glory of the Fatherland. . . . and where commerce is the source of public wealth, not simply the monstrous opulence of a few families.

Such was the ideal society portrayed in Jacobin books, newspapers, songs, images, and festivals. Some zealots were willing to accept dictatorship and bloodshed in the hope of realizing this ideal, but many people grew weary of the guillotine, price controls, bread lines, police informers, religious persecution, moral austerity, and the ban on luxury. In the circumstances they found the Jacobin promise of happiness on earth unconvincing.

In spite of its short duration and inherent weaknesses, the Jacobin program was by no means a complete failure. Although it failed to create *une volonté unique* and instead left France bitterly divided, it did contribute to arousing and sustaining a sort of religious fervour among many republicans at the height of the Revolution. Its adherents constituted a minority, but for a time they managed to make their faith into a sort of state religion. And although anti-Jacobinism triumphed after Thermidor, the Jacobin faith did not die out. It inspired radicalism throughout the world for more than a century, and its political program was almost completely enacted during the Third Republic. Moreover, its modes of thought survived in a hundred ways in nineteenth-century France. Flaubert's M. Homais, as Crane Brinton observes, was almost too good a Jacobin.

Above all, in their attempt at mass indoctrination the Jacobins carried western man to the threshold of modern times. We have seen that in their effort to break with the past they drew many assumptions and techniques from tradition—from age-old folk customs, from classical antiquity, from Christianity, from divine-right monarchy. But for all its traditional ingredients, the Jacobin campaign of indoctrination had an entirely new dimension, in intention if not in realization. As one examines Jacobin plans to saturate the environment with inspirational messages and behavioural models, one cannot help thinking of the mass rallies of Hitler's Germany, the art and theatre of Stalin's Russia, or the songs and catechisms of Mao's China. And in the West one thinks too of Madison Avenue and its messages which constantly assault our senses through every medium. There were portents of all these in Year II of the French Republic.

As we look back to 1794 we no longer share the optimism of the Jacobin as he stood on the threshold of modern times. For him the malleability of the human mind was a cause of hope because he was confident that the individual would be moulded in a desirable way. But we have not only witnessed the indoctrination of the totalitarian state and modern ad-men: we have read

George Orwell's *1984* and Vance Packard's *Hidden Persuaders* or watched Peter Watkins' movie *Privilege*. We can no longer be as confident as the Jacobin that the mass media, now so much more pervasive and powerful in an electronic age, will be used to enlighten man and create the good society.

FURTHER READING, LOOKING, AND LISTENING

There is no general account of propaganda inside France during the Terror, but there have been numerous specialized studies laying the basis for such an account although much research remains to be done. Only a few of the more important and accessible works can be listed since a complete bibliography would require a book in itself and many of the recent books cited here contain excellent bibliographies. In order to bring the media to life I have included pictures, slides, and records.

Among the best books providing political background are G. Lefebvre, *The French Revolution*, 2 vols., New York, 1962-1964; R. R. Palmer, *The Age of the Democratic Revolution*, 2 vols., Princeton, 1959-1964; L. Gershoy, *The French Revolution and Napoleon*, New York, 1964; G. Rudé, *Revolutionary Europe 1783-1815*, London, 1964; M. J. Sydenham, *The French Revolution*, London, 1965; and G. Ferrero, *The Two French Revolutions 1789-1796*, New York, 1968. W. B. Kerr, *The Reign of Terror 1793-1794* . . . , Toronto, 1927, is still one of the best general studies of the peak of the Revolution. On the Jacobins see C. Brinton, *The Jacobins: an Essay in the New History*, New York, 1930, reprint, 1961; G. Walter, *Histoire des Jacobins*, Paris, 1946; plus a brief outline by G. Martin, *Les Jacobins*, Paris, 1945. On the "revolutionary government" of Year II the classic study is R. R. Palmer, *Twelve Who Ruled: The Committee of Public Safety during the Terror*, Princeton, 1941, reprint 1965. For the most important government documents see J. H. Stewart, *A Documentary Survey of the French Revolution*, New York, 1951, and for an excellent selection of revolutionary thought, J. Godechot, *La Pensée révolutionnaire en France et en Europe*, Paris, 1964. A useful guide to recent literature is J. H. Stewart, *The French Revolution: Some Trends in Historical Writing*, 1945-1965, American Historical Association Service Centre for Teachers of History, Publication 67.

On books, pamphlets, and periodicals there is a variety of works, although much research remains to be done. P. Beurdeley, *Les Catéchismes révolutionnaires. Etude historique et péda-*

gogique sur la morale civique, Paris, 1894, treats only a limited selection of civic primers. H. Welschinger, *Les Almanachs de la Révolution*, Paris, 1884, is still a useful study. A. Söderhjelm, *Le Régime de la presse pendant la Révolution française*, 2 vols., Helsingsfors, 1900-1901, is good, though rather brief on the Terror. Among other informative histories of the revolutionary press are: L. E. Hatin, *Histoire politique et littéraire de la presse en France*, 8 vols., Paris, 1859-1861, vols. IV-VII; L. Gallois, *Histoire des journaux et des journalistes de la Révolution française*, 2 vols., Paris, 1845-1846; H. Avenel, *Histoire de la presse française depuis 1789 jusqu'à nos jours*, Paris, 1900; F. Mitton, *La Presse française*, vol. II, Paris, 1945; and R. de Livois, *Histoire de la presse française*, vol. I, Paris, 1965. Many more regional studies are needed on the model of R. Gérard, *Un Journal de province sous la Révolution. Le "Journal de Marseille"* . . . *1781-1797*, Paris, 1964. On subsidization of the press see A. Aulard, "La Presse officieuse pendant la Terreur", *Etudes et leçons sur la Révolution française*, 9 séries, Paris, 1893-1921, 1ère série, vol. I, pp. 227-240, and A. Mathiez, "La Presse subventionnée en l'an II", *Annales révolutionnaires*, vol. X, 1918, pp. 112-113.

On the theatre, M. Carlson, *The Theatre of the French Revolution*, Ithaca, 1966, provides an excellent summary of earlier studies by French scholars and a good selected bibliography, but deals only with Paris in spite of the title. Beatrice F. Hyslop, "The Theater during a Crisis: the Parisian Theater during the Reign of Terror", *The Journal of Modern History*, vol. XVII, Dec., 1945, pp. 332-355, analyses the most popular plays, discusses the new trends, and provides some interesting statistics. Other useful works include J.-A. Rivoire, *Le Patriotisme dans le théâtre sérieux de la Révolution, 1789-1799*, Paris, 1950, showing that "patriotism" embraced much more than narrow nationalism; K. McKee, *The Rôle of the Priest on the Parisian Stage during the French Revolution*, Baltimore, 1939, a revealing thesis not cited by Carlson; J. Hérissay, *Le Monde des théâtres pendant la Révolution*, Paris, 1922, containing many revealing documents; P. d'Estrée, *Le Théâtre sous la Terreur*, Paris, 1913, an excellent study; E. Lunel, *Le Théâtre et la Révolution*, Paris, 1911; H. Welschinger, *Le Théâtre de la*

Révolution, Paris, 1880; and E. Jauffret, *Le Théâtre révolutionnaire*, Paris, 1869. On provincial activity see, P. Courteault, *La Révolution et les théâtres à Bordeaux*, Paris, 1926; P. de Longuemare, *Le Théâtre à Caen, 1628-1830*, Paris, 1895; and J. Noury, *Le Théâtre-français à Rouen en 1793*, Rouen, 1893.

On the use of images as propaganda during the Terror see the fifth chapter of my monograph, *The Idea of Art as Propaganda in France 1750-1799: a Study in the History of Ideas*, Toronto, 1965. D. Dowd, "Art as National Propaganda in the French Revolution", *Public Opinion Quarterly*, Fall, 1951, pp. 532-546; " 'Jacobinism' and the Fine Arts: the Revolutionary Careers of Bouquier, Sergent, and David", *Art Quarterly*, vol. XVI, no. 3, 1953, pp. 195-214; and "The French Revolution and the Painters", *French Historical Studies*, vol. I, no. 2, 1959, pp. 127-148, are only a few of the author's valuable articles, others of which are listed in the bibliography in my book. Older studies include M. W. Brown, *The Painting of the French Revolution*, New York, 1938, a somewhat sketchy Marxist account; M. Dreyfous, *Les Arts et les artistes pendant la période révolutionnaire*, Paris, 1906, an outline of developments in the plastic arts, music, theatre, and festivals; S. Blondel, *L'Art pendant la Révolution*, Paris, 1887, a good summary; and J. Renouvier, *Histoire de l'art pendant la Révolution* ..., Paris, 1863, mainly a study of engravings. On cartoons see A. Blum, *La Caricature révolutionnaire*, Paris, 1917, and J. Fleury, *Histoire de la caricature sous la République, l'Empire, et la Restauration*, Paris, 1874. Crockery decorations have been treated by J. Fleury, *Histoire des faïences patriotiques sous la Révolution*, Paris, 1867. For reproductions see, in addition to many of the books above, F. Sieburg, *Im Licht und Schatten der Freiheit: Frankreich 1789-1848. Bilder und Texte*, Stuttgart, 1961; E. F. Henderson, *Symbol and Satire in the French Revolution*, London, 1912; A. Dayot, *La Révolution française . . . d'après des peintres, gravures, sculptures, estampes, médailles* ..., Paris, 1896; and the two volumes of plates appended to the *Réimpression de l'Ancien Moniteur*, 34 vols., Paris, 1849-1864. There is a fairly good set of slides in lecture 13 of the series "French Civilization as Reflected in the Arts" (Cultural History Research Inc., 6 Purchase St., Rye, New York).

On the music of the Revolution, Constant Pierre produced a series of studies back at the turn of the century: *Le Magasin de musique à l'usage des fêtes nationales*..., Paris, 1895, a study of the publishing centre established by the musicians of the Paris National Guard; *Musique des fêtes et cérémonies de la Révolution française*, Paris, 1899, a collection of some of the more important hymns and songs with the music adapted for piano; and *Les Hymnes et chansons de la Révolution*..., Paris, 1904, a list of hymns and songs of the period plus valuable historical and bibliographical notes. J. Tiersot, *Les Fêtes et les chants de la Révolution française*, Paris, 1908, is a lively and informative survey. The fourth volume of P. Barbier and F. Vernillat, *Histoire de France par les chansons*, 8 vols., Paris, 1956-1961, reproduces a selection of revolutionary songs with an historical commentary. My own article, "Music as an Ideological Weapon in the French Revolution", *The Canadian Historical Association Annual Report 1966*, Ottawa, 1967, pp. 126-140, is a fuller treatment of the theme of the sixth talk. Among the records available, nos. 8, 9, and 10 in the series *Histoire de France par les chansons*, Chant du monde, LDY 4108-10 bring to life some of the songs in the printed series with the same title by P. Barbier and F. Vernillat. A magnificent set of three long-playing disks, *La Révolution française*, Guilde internationale du disque, M 2263-1, 2, and 3, reproduces many of the speeches and songs of the epoch. Also worth mentioning are two records entitled *Chants et hymnes de la Révolution française*, Le Club français du disque, no. 261, and a single disk, *Chants révolutionnaires*, Chant du monde, LD 45-3001.

On festivals, D. Dowd, *Pageant-Master of the Republic: Jacques-Louis David and the French Revolution*, Lincoln, Nebraska, 1948, is an invaluable study, although very pro-Jacobin in tone. A. Blum, "Les fêtes républicaines et la tradition révolutionnaire", *La Révolution française*, vol. LXXII, 1919, pp. 193-200, is still worth consulting. A. Aulard, *Le Culte de la Raison et de l'Etre suprême*, Paris, 1885, and A. Mathiez, "Robespierre et le culte de l'Etre suprême", *Annales révolutionnaires*, 1910, pp. 209-238, are revealing studies of republican liturgy. For activities outside Paris see B. Blois, *Les Fêtes révolutionnaires à Angers de l'an II à l'an VII*, Paris, 1929; E. Charton,

Dix ans de fêtes nationales et de cérémonies publiques à Rouen 1790-1799, Paris, 1911; and M. Dommanget, "Le Symbolisme et le prosélytisme révolutionnaires à Beauvais et dans l'Oise", *Annales historiques de la Révolution française*, 1925, pp. 131-150, 1926, pp. 47-58 and 345-362, 1927, pp. 127-134. Also indispensable are the works by C. Pierre, J. Tiersot, cited above in the section on music, and by E. F. Henderson in the section on images.